AF541775

MULBERRY CROP PROTECTION
(CONCEPTS AND APPROACHES)

MULBERRY CROP PROTECTION
(CONCEPTS AND APPROACHES)

By

Tribhuwan Singh

Ph. D. (Entomology)
Deputy Director
Central Silk Board, Ministry of Textiles
Govt. of India
Research Extension Centre, Una
(Himachal Pradesh)
(India)

&

Pramod Kumar Singh

Ph.D. (School of Life Sciences)
Joint Director
Regional Sericultural Research Station
Central Silk Board, Ministry of Textiles
Govt. of India, Sahaspur
Dehradun (Uttarakhand)
(India)

DISCOVERY PUBLISHING HOUSE PVT. LTD.
NEW DELHI-110 002

Published by:
Tilak Wasan

DISCOVERY PUBLISHING HOUSE PVT. LTD.
4383/4B, Ansari Road, Darya Ganj
New Delhi-110 002 (India)
Phone : +91-11-23279245, 43596064-65
Fax : +91-11-23253475
E-mail : parul.wasan@gmail.com
discoverypublishinghouse@gmail.com
web : www.discoverypublishinggroup.com

***First Edition:* 2013**

ISBN: 978-93-5056-284-0

Mulberry Crop Protection
(Concepts and Approaches)

Printed at:
Dynamic Printers
Delhi

Preface

One of the unique contributions of the biology to mankind is the discovery of silk popularly known as the 'Queen of Textiles'. India enjoys the unique distinction of being the only country in the world to produce all four varieties of silk – Mulberry, Tasar, Eri and Muga and is the second largest producer of silk next only to China and has been recording consistent growth in the production. Silk is a proteinacious material 'par excellence' secreted by the lepidopteron sericigenous insect. The discovery of natural relationship between the two has led an idea of production of silk in systematic manner. In order to produce more and more silk, efforts have been made to exploit the relationship between the two to its logical end. As a result of this, many countries ventured to take-up the task by developing suitable methods and technologies leading to the birth of sericulture industry.

Mulberry (*Morus* sp.) is an important commercial crop grown extensively both in tropical and temperate countries of the world. As India encompasses wide geographical and agro-climatic variations, mulberry sericulture is distributed in temperate, sub-tropical and tropical regions, while the major share comes from the tropics. Its leaf protein is the main source for silkworm (*Bombyx mori*) to biosynthesize the silk fiber. Since the quality and quantity of silk depend on the quality of mulberry leaves hence good quality of mulberry leaves are essential for the production of good silk. Different components such as mulberry cultivation for production of quality mulberry leaves as a source of food for silkworm, improved method of silkworm rearing technology for healthy growth and development of larvae, silkworm egg production technology to maintain productivity and quality besides processing and reeling of cocoons have been well defined. As a result, country experienced a quantum jump in silk production and India has emerged as the second largest producer of silk in the world. In recent times, cocoon production has been considered as an important cash crop from the status of a very traditional and small subsidiary crop of marginal returns. Thanks are due to the pioneering efforts of Indian sericulture scientists to improve productivity per unit area. In fact, sericulture industry in India has been making steady and sustained progress through planned approaches. The current improvement in productivity and quality has made Indian sericulture highly attractive to the farmers.

Mulberry leaf is a major economic component in sericulture since the quality and quantity of leaf has a direct bearing on cocoon production and cocoon yield. There are many high yielding mulberry varieties with luxuriant biomass that have, in fact, changed the production equations; these high yielder blessed with good inputs and irrigation not only improved the national average leaf yield of mulberry but also transformed the very outlook of silkworm rearing activity into a professional one. Increased availability of leaves led to increase in rearing capacity at individual farmer's level paving way to expansion of infrastructure and absorption of improved technologies and techniques. Yet the diseases and pests have always been the limiting factor for mulberry cultivation and productivity, as they cause often considerable damage to mulberry crop and deteriorate the quality and quantity of mulberry leaf yield. The threats imposed by pests and diseases necessitate extreme care in handling of mulberry plant. In general, outbreak of diseases and pests causing continuous low leaf yield with poor qualitative and quantitative characters has been usual phenomenon associated with tropical sericulture. But when innumerable changes are taking place in the society, sericulture scientists cannot remain as a silent spectator and therefore studied their causal agents, symptoms, pathogenesis, mode and source of infection, predisposing factors, epidemiology, biology, management, prevention and control and published the results here and there in different forms. However, there is no updated compendium of information in sericulture on these aspects which relates to various strategies to be adopted for the prevention and control of pests and diseases of mulberry as well as forecasting of their occurrence in advance.

Therefore, it was thought desirable to publish a comprehensive book on the subject. This book is designed to address wide range of readers, experts, university teachers, students, researchers, technologists, policy makers and to fulfill the hopes and aspirations of all those engaged in sericulture. It will serve as a very useful guide and will motivate and assist in the efforts to find solutions to the existing problems in order to prevent and control the diseases and pests of mulberry to increase production, productivity and quality of leaf. It is very well established that 'an ounce of prevention is worth a pound of cure' and it may be three or more pounds true in management of mulberry diseases and pests. This book has many unique features. It comprises diseases of mulberry *viz.,* fungal diseases, bacterial diseases, viral diseases, mycoplasma disease, nematode disease besides diseases caused by deficiency and excess of minerals and adverse climatic conditions; pests of mulberry *viz.,* insect pests (mealy bug, whitefly, scale insect, caterpillar, defoliator etc.) and non-insect pest (snail, nematodes etc.) and its taxonomic position, distribution, biology, life span, prevention as well as control measures to achieve sustained and quality cocoons with increase production and productivity. A list of bio-pesticides banned for use in sericulture is also furnished. Surveillance and forecasting of pests and diseases is also included. The information furnished in this book will be of immense importance not only to Indian sericulture but also to South Asian and African countries and will find an application at all levels of sericulture.

To present the comprehensive and updated information in this book "*Mulberry Crop Protection – Concepts & Approaches*", we have drawn necessary information, photographs and scores from various published books, documents, periodicals, journals, technical reports etc., and help taken from all of them is gratefully acknowledged.

It is with great pleasure, we wish to express our sincere thanks to all those we had interactions and enlightened discussion which stimulated and prompted us to take up this onerous task of compiling all the available information on the pests and diseases of mulberry. We wish to place on records our profound thanks to all those friends and well wishers who have directly or indirectly helped in one way or the other and for the constant encouragement in bringing out this publication. A reliable guide and lovable compilation, this book is sure to appeal all those who are engaged in mulberry cultivation and holistic development of sericulture industry in the country.

We profoundly thank Sri Tilak Wasan, Director and Publisher, Discovery Publishing House, New Delhi whose interest and enthusiasm have brought out this book with an excellent presentation within a short period.

Though all-out efforts have been made to incorporate correct and authentic information, some errors might have crept inadvertently, please bring out such errors if any to the notice of the authors and publishers. Views and suggestions from users of this book are welcome to improve upon future editions.

Dr. Tribhuwan Singh
Dr. Pramod Kumar Singh

Contents

Behavioural control —(d) Biological control—(10) DEFOLIATOR (Diaphania pulveruntalis)—Taxonomic Position —Nature of Damage—Management —(11) CUT WORM (Spodoptera litura)—Taxonomic Position —Nature of Damage—Management —(12) BARK CATERPILLAR (Indarbela quadrinotata)—Taxonomic Position—Nature of Damage—Management—(13) RED HAIRY CATERPILLAR (Amsacta albistringa)—Taxonomic Position—Nature of Damage—Management—(14) MORINGA HAIRY CATERPILLAR (Eupterote mollifera)—Taxonomic Position—Nature of Damage—Management—(15) TUSSOCK CATERPILLAR (Euproctis fraterna)—Taxonomic Position—Nature of Damage—Management—(16) LOOPER (Hyposidra talaca)—Taxonomic Position—Nature of Damage —Management—(17) MULBERRY WEEVIL—Taxonomic Position—Nature of Damage—Management—Taxonomic Position—Nature of Damage—Management—(18) LONGHORN BEETLE (Batocera rufomaculata)—Taxonomic Position—Nature of Damage—Management—(19) LEAF BEETLE (Mimastra cyanura)—Taxonomic Position—Nature of Damage—Management—(20) CHAFER GRUBS (Schizonycha ruficallis)—Taxonomic Position—Nature of Damage—Management—(21) TERMITES (Odontotermus obsesus) —Taxonomic Position—Management —(22) STEM GIRDLER BEETLE (Sthenias grisator)—Taxonomic Position—Nature of Damage—Management—(23) STEM BORER (Apriona germarii)—Taxonomic Position—Nature of Damage—Management—(24) LONG-TAILED MEALYBUG (Pseudococcus longispinus)—Taxonomic Position—Nature of Damage—Management—(25) PAPAYA MEALYBUG (Paracoccus marginatus)—Taxonomic Position—Nature of Damage—Management—(26) GRASSHOPPERS (Neorthacris acuticeps

CHAPTER

Introduction

Sericulture has been promoted as an agro-based, labour intensive rural oriented cottage industry in the country, providing gainful employment mainly to the weaker and marginalized sections of the society. It is a highly remunerative occupation requiring little capital investment. It is estimated that sericulture can generate employment @11 man days per kg of raw silk production (in on-farm and off-farm activities) throughout the year. Silk being an exclusive fiber and popular as "Queen of Textiles", the money moves from the rich and urban market to the poor and rural producers. As sericulture is eco-friendly sustainable economic activity it checks migration of rural youths to urban areas. The developed countries as are retreating from the silk production in view of increased cost of human power, silk production provides hopes and opportunities to the developing countries. Having realized the benefits of investing resources in sericulture, the Union Government and the States over the years have laid emphasis on programmes based on sericulture for rural development. The role of sericulture and silk manufacturing industry in putting the country in its present position in the global scenario and the potential that exists for the agrarian economy like India, to further lead the world silk market owing to its rich diversity in respect of agro-climatic zones, diversity in the variety of silk that no single country can boast of, skilled manpower that creates magic out of this queen of textiles cannot be overlooked by any planner.

India is the second largest producer of silk in the World, next to China, and has 15.52 per cent share in global raw silk production. The World production of raw silk as on 2009 was 1,26,995 MT, China produces 1,04,000 MT being the first in the world. India produced 21,005 MT of silk (during 2010-11) which is the second largest producer in the world. Brazil, Thailand, Uzbekistan and Vietnam are also producing silk around 700 to 1000 MT in a year. India enjoys the unique distinction of being the only country in the world to produce all four varieties of silk—Mulberry, Tasar, Eri and Muga and is the second largest producer of silk next only to China and has been recording consistent growth in the production. As India encompasses wide geographical and agro-climatic variations, mulberry sericulture is distributed in temperate, sub-tropical and tropical regions, while the major share comes from the tropics. Mulberry (*Morus* sp.) is the sole food plant of the silkworm, (*Bombyx mori*). It is deep rooted, perennial, widely adaptable, high biomass producing and protein rich foliage plant with luxuriant growth which forms an unlimited source of food, nutrition, space and shelter for a variety of pests and diseases, causing considerable damage to the plant to varying degrees and intensities. Prevention and control of these, therefore, is an important part of sericulture activities. The availability of new production inputs such as cultivation of high yielding mulberry varieties, frequent irrigation, increased use of Farm Yard Manure (FYM) and fertilizers etc. have led to keep mulberry at its growing stage throughout the year and hence providing congenial conditions for the continuity of pests and diseases in the host plant.

Monocultures, overlapping crop seasons due to overlapping pruning schedules and excessive application of chemical fertilizers and irrigation water have led to severe outbreaks of pests. So far, more than 300 species of insects and other organisms have been reported to cause damage to mulberry from different mulberry growing countries, of which over 50 pests are known to cause significant loss. Frequent leaf picking and pruning of shoots, though restricts the incidence of pests, many of them find enough time and space on mulberry for their feeding and shelter. The damage caused by the pest is often quick and extensive. Lepidopteran pests, thrips and mites cause considerable damage to mulberry crop. The attack by these pests is sporadic and sometimes seasonal. The climatic factors play substantial role in the biology of any pest, of which temperature is, the most crucial abiotic factor influencing the life cycle of any organism. The extent of damage varies with type of pest and season. The damage is caused by either larval or nymphal or adult stage of the insect. Mulberry is also subjected to damage by various species of sap sucking and foliage feeding insects. In all, 30 species are recorded to inflict damage to the mulberry leaves by sucking.

Diseases have always been the major constraint in mulberry cultivation, the intensity of which varies with season, variety and cultivation practices. Mulberry is grown under wide range of ecological conditions. During the growth, like any other plant, various types of pathogens causing diseases such as fungi, bacteria, mycoplasma, viruses and nematodes also affect mulberry. Diseases, which are the main constraints in leaf production, are caused either by pathogens or non-pathogens. Among pathogens, leaf spot (fungal and bacterial), powdery mildew, leaf rust and root knot are most common diseases, which cause economically significant loss. Foliar diseases of mulberry affect leaf yield as well as leaf quality resulting in poor cocoon crop and consequent reduction in the income of the seri-farmers. Leaf yield loss due to leaf spot, powdery mildew and leaf rust disease has been reported to be the tune of 46.8 per cent, 20.45 per cent and 17.35 per cent respectively during the respective damaging seasons. Besides, these diseases also affects leaf quality leading to poor silkworm rearing and crop loss up to 54.58 per cent and 55.59 per cent at maximum severity of leaf spot and powdery mildew respectively. Diseased mulberry leaves are poor in proteins, sugars and moisture. As most of the farmers in India are marginal and small farmers having limited land holding, the loss due to the diseases cannot be underestimated and therefore appropriate plant protection measures are necessary to boost effectively mulberry foliage production. Non-infectious or non-pathogenic or physiological diseases are caused by mineral excess or mineral deficiency in the soil, unfavourable temperature, moisture, air pollution etc. These diseases remain non-infectious and are not transmitted from one plant to another healthy plant.

It is necessary to familiarize one-self with the principles underlying the initiation, development and spread of these diseases, to identify, prevent or cure to obtain quality leaf. A number of reviews, handbooks and bulletins are available to describe pests and diseases of mulberry on certain specific lines or as a part of book chapters. However, these are inadequate to reflect pests and diseases properly in order to enrich the knowledge of seri-farmers, students, researches, policy-makers etc.

This book therefore, provides comprehensive details of pests and diseases of mulberry and their management, written to cater to the specific needs of Indian States. This publication aims at serving the basic needs of seri-farmers *i.e.,* production of healthy mulberry leaf for harvesting stable cocoon crop and quality silk. This as a reference book will be of immense help to the students and teachers of sericulture; to the scientists working in laboratories and in the field; to the sericulture extension workers and for general academic/ professional interest. Attempts have been made to—

- Discuss the major and minor pests of mulberry found

in Indian States, their systematic position, distribution, pest status, seasonal incidence and nature of damage, biology and management practices.

- Discuss the major and minor diseases of mulberry found in Indian States, their seasonal incidence, symptoms, pathogen and diseases cycle and management practices.
- Discuss abiotic factors induced disorders of mulberry and their management.
- Discuss briefly the forecasting system of pests and diseases of mulberry.
- Discuss briefly the integrated disease management, some tips on use of pesticides and list of commonly used and banned pesticides.

Mulberry Pests

India encompasses wide geographical and agro-climatic variations. Accordingly, mulberry sericulture is distributed in temperate, sub-tropical and tropical regions, while the major share comes from the tropics. Mulberry (*Morus* sp.) of the family Moraceae, the primary food plant of the silkworm, *Bombyx mori*) is deep rooted, perennial, widely adaptable, high biomass producing and protein rich foliage plant with luxuriant growth which, forms an unlimited source of food, nutrition, space and shelter for a variety of pests, causing considerable damage to the plant to varying degrees and intensities. Monocultures, overlapping crop seasons due to overlapping pruning schedules and excessive application of chemical fertilizers and irrigation water have led to severe outbreaks of pests. So far, more than 300 species of insects and other organisms have been reported to cause damage to mulberry from different mulberry growing countries, of which over 50 pests are known to cause significant loss (Kotikal, 1982; Biradar, 1989). Frequent leaf picking and pruning of shoots, though restricts the incidence of pests, many of them find enough time and space on mulberry for their feeding and shelter. The damage caused by the pest is often quick and extensive. Lepidopteran pests, thrips and mites cause considerable damage to mulberry crop. The attack by these pests is sporadic and sometimes seasonal. The climatic factors play substantial role in the biology of any pest, of which temperature is, the most crucial abiotic factor influencing the life cycle of any organism. The extent of damage varies with type of pest and season. The damage is caused by either larval or nymphal or adult stage of the insect. Further, in some cases, damage caused by these pests is observed throughout the year. Some of these pests eat leaves and check the growth of mulberry plants or they live as parasite on shoots.

Mulberry is subjected to damage by various species of sap sucking and foliage feeding insects. In all, 30 species were recorded to inflict damage to the mulberry leaves by sucking. Among the sapsuckers, 18 Heteropteran, 10 Homopteran and 2 Thysanopteran species are reported. Among the defoliators, 18 species (13 Lepidopteran, 3 Coleopteran and 2 Orthopteran) inflict damage to mulberry leaves by chewing.

Some of the important pests are summarized in Table 2.1 and Table 2.2.

Table 2.1 : Pest of Mulberry Reported from India

Sl. No.	Pests	Season	Region
1.	**Mealy bug** *Maconellicoccus hirsutus*	Summer	Throughout the country
2.	**Long-tailed mealy bug** *Pseudococcus longispinus*	Summer	Southern region
3.	**Papaya mealy bug** *Paracoccus marginatus*	Summer	Southern region
4.	**Whitefly** *Dialeuropora decempuncta*	July & August	Eastern region
5.	**Spiralling whitefly** *Aleurodicus disperses*	All seasons	Throughout the country

Sl. No.	Pests	Season	Region
6.	**Scale insects** *Saissetia nigra, Pulvenaria maxima, Aonidiella aurantii*	Summer	Throughout the country
7.	**Hairy caterpillar** *Spilarctia casignata*	All seasons	Temperate region
8.	**Leaf caterpillar** *Margaronia pyloalis*	Summer & rainy	Temperate region
9.	**Bihar hairy caterpillar** *Spilosoma obliqua*	Summer	Throughout the country
10.	**Defoliator** *Diaphinia pulveruntalis*	Summer	Karnataka and Tamil Nadu
11.	**Tobacco caterpillar** *Spodoptera litura*	All seasons	Throughout the country
12.	**Bark Caterpillar** *Inderbela quadrinotata, Apriona germarri*	All seasons	Karnataka, Andhra Pradesh & Tamil Nadu
13.	**Red hairy caterpillar** *Amsacta albistriga*	Summer & rainy	Karnataka, Tamil Nadu & Andhra Pradesh
14.	**Moringa hairy caterpillar** *Eupterote mollifera*	Winter & summer	Throughout the country
15.	**Tussock caterpillar** *Euproctis fraternal*	Summer	Karnataka, Andhra Pradesh & Tamil Nadu

Sl. No.	Pests	Season	Region
16.	**Looper** *Hyposidra talaca*	Summer & rainy	Throughout the country
17.	**Wasp caterpillar** *Amata passalis, Ceryx godarti*	Summer	Throughout the country
18.	**Thrips** *Pesudodendrothrips mori*	Rainy	Throughout the country
19.	**Stem girdler** *Sthenias grisator*	All seasons	Throughout the country
20.	**Stem borer** *Lassioglossum* sp.	Summer & rainy	Karnataka, Andhra Pradesh & Tamil Nadu
21.	**Mulberry weevils** *Episomus fungulus, Myllocerus dentifer, M. discolor, M. viridianus, M. dorsatus*	Summer	Throughout the country
22.	**Cockchafer beetle** *Holotrichia* sp.	Summer	Karnataka & Tamil Nadu
23.	**Longicorn beetle** *Batocera rufomaculata Apriona germarii*	May-June	Jammu
24.	**Leaf beetle** *Maladera insanabilis*	June-July	Jammu
25.	**Chafer grubs** *Schizonicha ruflcollis*	Summer & rainy	Temperate region
26.	**Leafhoppers (Jassids)** *Empoasca flavescens, Batrocomophus angus-*	Rainy	Karnataka, Andhra

Sl. No.	Pests	Season	Region
	tatus, Kolla clylonica, Neodartus acocephsloides, Empoasca decipens, Asymmetrasca decedens		Pradesh & Tamil Nadu
27.	**Termites** *Coptotermus heimi, Odontotermus guptai, Odontotermus obesus, Microtermus obesi*	Summer	Throughout the country
28.	**Wingless grasshopper** *Neorthacris acuticeps nilgriensis*	Rainy	Throughout the country
29.	**Mites** *Tetranychus equitorius, T. telanius, T. kanzawari, Cotetranychus suginamensis, Polyphagotarsonemus latus*	Winter & summer	Throughout the country
30.	**Red weaver ant** *Oecophylla smaragdina*	All seasons	Through out the country
31.	**Blister beetle** *Lepidiota bimaculata*	June-July	Jammu
32.	**Tortix moth** *Archips subsidiaria*	Summer	Karnataka
33.	**Hawk moth** *Acherontia* sp.	November	South India
34.	**Leaf beetle** *Mimastra cyanura*	Rainy	Throughout the country
35.	**Leaf Webber** *Glyphodes pyloalis*	Rainy season	West Bengal
36.	**Leaf hoppers** *Batracomorphus angustatus*	Rainy	Karnataka & Tamil Nadu

Sl. No.	Pests	Season	Region
37.	**Snails** *Cochilopa* sp.*Cyclophorus fulguratus, Acrtaustenia ovata*	Winter	Throughout the country
38.	**Nematodes** *Meloidogyne incognita, M. javanica, Xiphinima basiri, Rotylenchus reniformis, Haplolumus indicus, Hemicriconemoides communis*	All seasons	Throughout the country

Table 2.2 : Pests of Mulberry not Reported from India

Sl. No.	Pest	Country
1.	**Span worm** *Pathonandria atrillaneta*	Burma, China, Japan, Korea, Vietnam
2.	**Leaf tier** *Diaphania pyloalis*	China
3.	**Clear-winged moth** *Paradoxecia pieli*	China
4.	**White caterpillar** *Rondotia menciana*	China
5.	**Brown tall moth** *Euproctis similes xanthocampa*	China
6.	**Mulberry weevil** *Baris deplanata*	China, Japan, Korea
7.	**Mulberry tiger moth** *Spilarctia imparillis*	Japan
8.	**Fall web worm** *Hyphantria cunea*	North America

S. No.	Pests	Season	Region
9.	**Mulberry looper** *Hemerophila atrilineata*		China, Japan
10.	**Mulberry leaf beetle** *Flentiauxia armata*		Japan
11.	**Mulberry flea beetle** *Luperomorpha funesta*		Japan
12.	**Mulberry sucker** *Anomoneura mori*		Japan
13.	**Leaf weevil** *Baris deplanata*		Japan, Indonesia
14.	**Rhombic-marked leaf hopper** *Hishimonus sellatus* **Hishimon-Modoki leaf hopper** *H. sellatiformis*		Japan
15.	**Wide-pitch scale** *Pseudaulacapsis pentagon*		Japan
16.	**Mulberry borer** *Apricona japonica*		Japan
17.	**Yellow-spotted longhorn beetle** *Psacothea kilaris*		Japan
18.	**Bark beetle** *Crypnanus exignus*		Japan
19.	**Wire worm** *Agriotes sericeus*		Japan
20.	**Nematodes** *Meloidogyne arenaria, M. mali*		Japan
21.	**Leaf roller** *Margaronia pulverulentalis*		Malaysia
22.	**Mulberry mealy bug** *Drosicha contrahens*		China, Thailand
23.	**Cricket** *Brachytrupes portentosus echlenetein*		Vietnam
24.	**Thrips** *Pseudodendrothrips* sp		Bangladesh

The important pests, their status, symptoms, extent of damage, seasonal occurrence and management practices are summarized briefly in the following text.

[A] INSECT PESTS

(1) MEALY BUG (*Maconellicoccus hirsutus)*

Maconellicoccus hirsutus (Green) is commonly called as mealy bug, pink mealy bug or hibiscus mealy bug or greenvine mealy bug.

Taxonomic Position

Phylum	:	Arthropoda
Class	:	Insecta
Order	:	Homoptera
Family	:	Pseudococcidae
Genus	:	*Maconellicoccus*
Species	:	*hirsutus* (Green)

Status of the pest: It is a major pest and popularly known as 'hard to kill' pest. The mealy bug has become an increasing threat to mulberry in recent years. It occurs in more than 13 tropical and sub-tropical countries of the world. However, the pest is widely distribution in Asia, Africa, Australasia, Pacific Islands, West Indies and North America. It is a polyphagous insect infesting more than 125 species in various zoogeographical regions (Ghosh, 1972), of which 28 are reported from India alone (Mani *et al.*, 1987; Mani, 1989) including mulberry, lady's finger, china rose, jute, grape vine, guava etc (Manjunath, 1985). Its wide host range favours rapid spread and make the control measures difficult. Although, the first report of *M. hirsutus* in association with mulberry dates back to 1908, serious qualitative and quantitative loss has been observed only in recent years, especially in Karnataka, Andhra Pradesh and Tamil Nadu, which together produces over 80 per cent of raw silk in India.

Biology: After mating, females deposit 350 -500 eggs in a white waxy ovisac. Eggs are elongated and orange in colour. The incubation period is 6-9 days. The nymphs are active crawlers. Male nymphs moult thrice, whereas females moult twice. Nymphal stage is very important, as this is the stage at which the pest spreads from one plant to the other or from one crop to the other. Nymphal period lasts for 23-27 days. Females have three while male have four nymphal instars. Adult exhibits sexual dimorphism. Males are black, slender and winged forms, whereas, females are pink, broader and lack wings. The male's longevity is 3-4 days while female survives for 10-12 days. The adults do not feed. The female dies in 2-3 days after oviposition. They also reproduce parthenogenetically. The adults are small about 2-3 mm in length and pink in body colour, covered with waxy secretion. Both nymphs and adults suck the sap from tender shoots and leaves causing loss in leaf yield. As many as 15 generations are there in a year. Manjunath *et al.* (1996) described the biology of mealy bug in detail.

Seasonal incidence: Mealy bug infestation of mulberry occurs throughout the year. However, they attain the status of pest from March-August. Peak infestation can be observed during April-June.

Alternative host plant: It is a dangerous pest of many plant species including trees and shrubs. So far, 346 host plants have been recorded for the pest. The major host plants are *Hibiscus*, citrus, coffee, sugarcane, guava, mango, teak, pigeon pea, grapevine, maize, beans, cotton, soybean etc. Its wide host range favours its rapid spread and makes its control difficult.

Nature of Damage

- Nymphs suck the plant sap from meristematic region and tender leaves.
- The affected apical shoot shows retarded growth, which tremendously affects the yield and quality of mulberry leaf besides nutritive value.

- Leaves curl at growing tips, become dark green in colour giving a leathery appearance.
- The stem thickened and twisted with shortening of inter-nodal distance and gives bunchy top appearance of plants. This symptom is generally called as 'tukra'.
- Leaves become yellow and fall premature.
- A heavy black sooty mould may develop on the leaves and stem due to heavy honeydew secretions by the mealy bug.
- Depletion in quality, nutritive value and quantity of leaves results in lower returns per unit area.
- Feeding tukra infested mulberry leaves results in reduction in economic characters of silkworm also. The Economic Threshold Level (ETL) value for mealy bug is 10 individuals/plant.

Management: Due to wide host range, habitat and adaptations, the pink mealy bug is regarded as 'hard to kill pest'. The Integrated management of mealy bug (Katiyar *et al.*, 2001) includes cultural/mechanical, chemical and biological methods.

Cultural/mechanical control: Clipping of tukra infested apical shoots and destruction by burning or burying during the initial stages of the infestation so that further spread and damage can be minimized. Alternate host plants such as croton, hibiscus, guava, grapes, lady's finger, cotton etc. should not be grown in the vicinity of mulberry garden.

Chemical control: Spraying of 0.2% DDVP (76% EC) for 2 to 3 times with 10 days interval is recommended. Safe period for use of mulberry leaves, as feed to the silkworm is 17 days after last spray.

Biological control: Release of @ 600 pairs of the predator, *Pullus bourdilloni* (Kapur) (Coleoptera: Coccinellidae) for Eastern and North-Eastern parts of India, and release of an exotic predator *Cryptolaemus montrouzieri* (Mulsant) @ 250 adult beetles/acre in two split dosages (October-November and January-February) is recommended for South India. The larvae and adults of these predators feed on all life stages of mealy bug without causing any harm to mulberry plantation.

An Integrated Pest Management (IPM) programme to check the mealy bug population is more effective. The following are the components of IPM in managing the mealy bug in mulberry garden :

- Weeds such as *Phyllanthus niruri, Clitoria ternatea, Chrchrous* sp. etc, harbour the mealy bugs. Such weeds should be removed from mulberry garden and destroyed.
- Severely infested mulberry stem tips should be removed and collected in a sac or basket and burnt.
- Mass release of coccinellid predator, *Cryptolaemus montrouzieri* @ 750/ha or *Scymnus coccivore* @ 500 adults/acre is quite effective to control mealy bug population.
- Spray 0.2 per cent DDVP (Nuvan) on pruned/leaf harvested plants 2-3 times at 10-12 days intervals. The spray mixture should be prepared in 0.5 per cent soap solution and applied. Leaves can be fed to silkworms after 17 days of last application.
- Ants play an important role in spreading mealy bugs in mulberry plantation. Nests of these ants should be located in and around mulberry plantation and treat those with 0.5 per cent Malathion dust just after pruning or leaf harvest.

(2) WHITEFLY (*Dialeuropora decempuncta)*

Whiteflies ranks among the most noxious insects attacking agricultural and ornamental crops besides green house crops around the world. Whitefly, *Dialeuropora decempuncta* (Quaintance & Baker) is polyphagous and serious pest of mulberry causing great economic loss by reducing the leaf yield in various parts of the country in general and

West Bengal and Assam in particular (Bandyopadyay *et al.*, 2001). The name whitefly is derived from the white appearance of the adults and their tendency to fly readily when disturbed. Singh *et al.* (2005) described biocenology and control of white-flies in sericulture.

Taxonomic Position

Phylum	:	Arthropoda
Class	:	Insecta
Order	:	Homoptera
Family	:	Aleyrodidae
Super family	:	Aleurodicinae
Genus	:	*Dialeuropora*
Species	:	*Decempuncta* (Q & B).

Status of the pest: This is a major mulberry pest distributed in Australia, Austro-oriental and Pacific regions and widely found in India, Pakistan and Sri Lanka. In India it was first reported from Lucknow on *Ficus religiosa* seedlings and later reported from different parts of the country. Whiteflies have wide range of alternate hosts belonging to horticultural, ornamental, trees and weed plants (Bandyopadyay and Santha Kumar, 2003). Some of the important alternate host plants are presented in Table 2.3.

Biology: The life cycle consists of egg, four nymphal instars and a pupal and adult stage. Though sexual reproduction is common, parthenogenesis also occurs from time to time. The eggs are elliptical, straw coloured, smooth and shiny lay singly and distributed all over ventral surface of the leaf through pedicel. The egg measures 0.21 mm long and 0.09 mm wide. Incubation period ranges from 10-16 days depending on the prevailing atmospheric temperature. The nymphs are oval in shape, reddish yellow in colour, body measures 0.92 mm × 0.06 mm. The young nymphs are crawlers and move about for a short time to settle down at a suitable place on the under surface of the leaves and loose their legs during the first moult. Second and third instar nymphs are sedentary, do not move and possess an elongated-oval body. The fourth instar nymph is generally considered as pupa with opaque—white body, which possess red coloured eyes. The nymphal stage lasts for 11-25 days. After completion of development, the adult whitefly comes out of the pupal case through an inverted 'T' shaped moulting suture leaving the pupal case on the leaf surface. The adults are minute and white in colour, measure 2 mm in length. They have a pair of equal floury wings, covered with whitish waxy powder; distinct compound eyes, well-developed thorax, abdomen ovate, moderately long legs and males possess short genetalia. Females are generally bigger than males. The life cycle is completed in about 30-41 days depending on the ambient temperature. It is longest during December-January *i.e.,* 55-60 days and shortest during March-April (25-35 days).

Table 2.3 : Alternate Host Plants of Whitefly

S.No.	Host plants	Family
1.	*Abelomoschus esculentus*	Malvaceae
2.	*Terminalia cattappa*	Combretaceae
3.	*Tectoma grandis*	Verbenaceae
4.	*Gossypium herbaceum*	Malvaceae
5.	*Abutilon indicum, Hibiscus rosasinensis*	Malvaceae
6.	*Pongamia pinnata, Bauhinia racemosa*	Fabaceae
7.	*Carica papaya*	Carricaceae
8.	*Psidium guava, Murraya coenigii*	Malvaceae
9.	*Annona squamosa*	Annonaceae
10.	*Citrus limon*	Rutaceae
11.	*Punica granatum*	Punicaceae
12.	*Justicia* sp.	Acanthaceae
13.	*Crossandra infudibuliformis*	Acanthaceae
14.	*Ficus* sp.	Moraceae

S.No.	Host plants	Family
15.	*Jasminum grandiflorum*	Oleaceae
16.	*Rosa indica*	Rosaceae
17.	*Vigna radiata, V. sinensis*	Fabaceae
18.	*Ipomoea batatus*	Convolvuaceae
19.	*Cucumis sativus*	Cucurbitaceae
20.	*Solanum melongena*	Solanaceae
21.	*Lycopersicon esculentum*	Solanaceae
22.	*Capsicum annum*	Solanaceae
23.	*Helianthus annus*	Compositae
24.	*Dolichos lablab*	Fabaceae
25.	*Phaseolus vulgaris*	Fabaceae
26.	*Solanum tuberosum*	Solanaceae

Seasonal incidence: Whitefly is found throughout the year, with its abundance during June-December and peak during September-October. The occurrence is more severe in irrigated mulberry gardens. The incidence of whitefly fluctuates depending on biotic and abiotic factors.

Nature of Damage

- Both adult and nymphal stages cause damage to mulberry.
- They insert long stylets into the phloem tissue and suck the sap, which results in chlorosis, loss of nutritive value and pre-mature leaf fall. Extensive sucking of phloem sap from the lower surface of the leaves causes upward curling and reduction in leaf yield (Bandyopadyay *et al.*, 2000).
- Damage due to infestation leads to yellowing and stunted growth.
- Whitefly is a potential vector of leaf curl virus causing leaf curl disease.

- The honeydew secreted by nymphs serves as a medium for the growth of sooty mould fungus (*Chaetothyrium* sp. and *Curvularia affinis)* causing sooty mould disease resulting in major crop loss.
- Feeding whitefly infested mulberry leaves to silkworm causes depletion in qualitative and quantitative parameters of silkworm.
- The leaf yield loss due to whitefly infestation is estimated to be about 23 per cent.
- The Economic Threshold Level (ETL) value for whitefly is 20 individuals/leaf (2nd/3rd leaf) (Bandyopadyay *et al.*, 2002). Beyond this level appropriate measure has to be taken to prevent substantial crop loss.

Swarm of whiteflies on mulberry leaves

Management

- Removal of whitefly infected ground level flora in proximity to mulberry plantation.
- Removal and burning of infested plant parts/dried leaves of other plants.

- Suppressing whitefly populations before they reach large numbers is essential to prevent plant damage.
- Weeds harbouring whitefly near the mulberry field *viz., Solanum indicum, Solanum nigra* etc. should be eradicated.
- Encourage application of VAM, Azotobacter and other bio-fertilizer to reduce the use of nitrogenous fertilizers.
- Spraying of 0.01 per cent Monocrotophos will be able to control whitefly infestation (Bandyopadyay *et al.*, 1999a). Safe period for use of mulberry leaves for feeding to silkworm is 15 days after spray.
- Horticultural oil and insecticidal soaps may provide control of low-density populations.
- Spray neem oil or neem products at the concentration of 5 ml/litre of water (Bandyopadyay and Santha Kumar, 2000).
- Use eco-friendly measures like sticky yellow traps @ 60/acre (size 2′ × 1′) at the borders of the mulberry plantations. It reduces the whitefly infestation to the tune of 25 per cent.
- Insect Growth Regulators (IGRs) must be applied more frequently, especially in situations where adults are abundant.
- Biological control of whitefly could be achieved by releasing *Micraspis discolor, Micraspis crocea, Brumus suturalis, Serangium percesetosa* that pray on both the nymphs and pupae of the whitefly. Parasitoids like *Encarsia dialeuroporae* and *Eccarsia longivalvula* are effective to kill nymphs of whitefly (Verranna, 1998).
- Use of microbial insecticide that contains the enteropathogenic fungus, *Beauvaria bassina,* can be avoided for whitefly suppression since this also kills the silkworm.

- Saw dust mulching reduces whitefly population due to its lethal action.
- Six rows of sun hemp or maize as border crops should be planted as trap crop with the application of Dimethoate (0.05%).

(3) SPIRALLING WHITEFLY (*Aleurodicus disperses*)

Aleurodicus disperses commonly known, as spiralling whitefly is a polyphagous and serious pest of mulberry and has an extensive host range, which includes mango, custard apple, papaya, sweet potato, cassava, avocado, colocasia, banana, guava, citrus, capsicums, brinjal, tomato, papaya, pepper, rose etc. The name spiralling is derived as it lays eggs in a typical spiral pattern.

Taxonomic Position

Phylum	:	Arthropoda
Class	:	Insecta
Order	:	Homoptera
Family	:	Aleyrodidae
Super family	:	Aleurodicinae
Genus	:	*Aleurodicus*
Species	:	*disperses* (Russell).

Status of the pest: Spiralling whitefly is considered a serious pest of tropical and sub-tropical regions.

Biology: Female spiralling whitefly laid 40-70 eggs on the underside of young leaves in a characteristic spiralling oviposition pattern. Incubation period is 4-6 days. Once hatched, first instars are mobile and disperse over the underside of the leaf. Subsequent instars are immobile and are also found on the underside of older leaves. The immobile instars range in size from 0.5 mm to 1.5 mm and produce waxy filaments and copious quantities of honeydew. The final instar is the pupa from which the adult fly emerges. The adult fly is approximately 2 mm long, with a white powdery wax over the wings and body. Life cycle completes in approximately 3 weeks during summer. The characteristic oviposition spirals are often only seen on recent infestations as wax and sooty mould production soon obscures the spirals.

Seasonal incidence: It is reported to cause damage throughout the year with high incidence in summer (March - June) and low in winter (October-January). The population is positively correlated with temperature and negatively with humidity.

Nature of Damage

- Immature and adult stages cause direct feeding damage by sucking plant sap, which results in chlorosis, yellowing, upward curling of the leaves and immature leaf fall.
- The nymphs and adults remain on the lower surface of the leaves and de-sap the plants. Continuous feeding weakens the plants.
- Direct damage is due to feeding by the insect on the plant phloem. They remove plant sap reducing plant vigour and growth. If the population of spiralling white fly per plant is considerable high, the plant may die.
- Indirect damage is due to the heavy production of honeydew and white waxy material produced by the insect. Sooty mould develops on honeydew and decreases photosynthetic activity.

Management

- Collection and destruction of infested leaves.
- Adoption of recommended package of practices of mulberry maintenance *viz.,* fertilizer doses, spacing, irrigation, training of plants etc.
- Use of coloured sticky traps in the field reduces pest population effectively.

- Spraying of 0.05 per cent Dimethoate 30 EC and 0.5 per cent neem oil mixed with 1 to 2 ml soap solution at 1:2 ratios. Safe period 7 days after spraying.
- Predators *Menochilus sexmaculatus* @ 200 adults per acre, *Cryptolaemus montrouzieri* @ 300 adults per acre and *Scymnus coccivora* @ 500 adults per acre can be used as biological control agents to minimize the pest.

(4) SCALE INSECT

(i) Saissetia nigra: *Saissetia nigra* is commonly known as black scale insect or unarmoured scales. Citrus, croton, chrysanthemum and banana are the alternate hosts for the scale insects. Apart from this, 13 species are reported from Pakistan followed by 9 in India, 5 each in Japan and USA and 4 in Israel (Oda, 1963; Datta, 1981; Narayanaswamy and Reddy, 1997).

Taxonomic Position

Class	:	Insecta
Order	:	Himiptera
Family	:	Coccidae
Genus	:	*Saissetia*
Species	:	*nigra* (Nietm).

Status of the pest: It is a minor pest damaging mulberry crop throughout the year but severe during summer. It is more prevalent in hilly regions of the country.

Biology: The female of *S. nigra* lays 300-600 eggs, which are minute, white and elongated. The colour of egg becomes reddish-brown with the advancement in age. The eggs hatch within 5-6 days. Nymphs start crawling and feeding within few hours after hatching. Nymphal period is 19-28 days. The nymphs secrete a fibrous waxy material, which hardens to form the scale. The female moults three times while the male twice. In the process of moulting they lose the appendages.

This makes them sedimentary in nature. Adult male survives for 6-11 days and female 9-18 days. The affected shoot is studded with thousands of dark brown or black scales. Reproduction takes place parthenogenetically.

Seasonal incidence: Incidence of the pest occurs during summer months on mulberry stem especially in tree and high bush type plantation.

Nature of Damage

- They suck the sap of the plants and affected shoots start dying from the distal end.
- Yellowish or mottled appearance of the leaf blade can also be noticed. They are usually found on the underside of leaves and stems. Scales on stems usually prefer new succulent shoots.
- The infected shoots are studded with hundreds of dark brown or black scales, which are the sedentary nymphs covered with their own secretion of fibrous waxy coat that hardens to form the scale. Honeydew like substance is also secreted allowing sooty mould to develop.

Scale insect

Management

- Infected portion should be cut and burnt.
- Swabbing with a blunt edge wooden plate to dislodge the insect.
- Swabbing of washing powder solution on the stem to dislodge the scale insect.
- Use of predators, such as the green lacewing and parasitic encirtid wasps.
- Spraying of 0.05 per cent Dimethoate with a ten days safe period.
- Spraying of Lime Sulphur solution on stem.
- Spray of 0.05 per cent Malathion with safe period of 10 days controls *S. nigra* on mulberry.
- In case of severe attack, a combination of Phosmet (19 ml), Malathion (6 ml) and DDVP (4 ml) in 10 litres of water should be prepared and sprayed twice at an interval of seven days with safe period of 10 days.

(ii) Pulvinaria maxima: *Pulvinaria maxima* are popularly known as soft scale insect. Its presence has been reported from India and Thailand.

Taxonomic Position

Class	:	Insecta
Order	:	Himiptera
Family	:	Coccidae
Genus	:	*Pulvinaria*
Species	:	*maxima* (Gr.).

Status of the pest: It is a minor pest damaging mulberry crops throughout the country. It is more prevalent and serious pest in hilly regions of the country.

Biology: The eggs are laid beneath the body of the mature female in a conspicuous egg sac, where upon the female dies.

As with other scale insects, the first instar nymph (crawler) is the active discursive phase responsible for starting new infestation. The adults are shield-shape, oval and 2-3 mm in body length.

Seasonal incidence: They damage the mulberry crops throughout the year. However, the peak the incidence is observed during summer months.

Nature of Damage

- Young shoots and tender leaves are mostly affected.
- Affected leaves gradually wilt.
- Honey dew secreted by the insect cause sooty mould formation on the lower leaves.
- Leathery brown females and small males, puparium are also seen on the stem or leaves of the infected plants.

Management

- Prune the infested shoots and burn them.
- Swabbing with a blunt edge wooden plate to dislodge the insect.
- Spraying of 0.05 per cent Dimethoate with a ten days safe period.
- Spraying of Lime Sulphur solution on stem.
- Swabbing of washing powder solution on the stem to dislodge the scale insect.
- Spray of 0.05 per cent Malathion with safe period of 10 days.
- Use of predators, such as the green lacewing and parasitic encirtid wasps.
- In case of severe attack, a combination of Phosmet (19 ml), Malathion (6 ml) and DDVP (4 ml) in 10 litres of water should be prepared and sprayed twice at an interval of seven days with safe period of 10 days.

(iii) Aonidiella aurantii: *Aonidiella aurantii* is popularly known as red scale insect. Its presence has been reported from India and Vietnam.

Taxonomic Position

Class	:	Insecta
Order	:	Himiptera
Family	:	Coccidae
Genus	:	*Aonidiella*
Species	:	aurantii (Maskell)

Status of the pest: They damage the mulberry crops throughout the year. However, the peak the incidence is observed during summer months in hilly regions.

Biology: The red scales are born at the average rate of 2-3 in a day for a period of two months during warmer months. The first instar crawlers have well developed legs and antennae and move about for an hour before settling. During this period, they begin to cover themselves with a white waxy covering. The female moults twice at 10-20 days interval, loses its legs and antennae and incorporates its cast skin into the waxy covering and hence becomes circular, depressed and reddish in colour. The female rotates while forming the scale covering. They mature in 2-3 months and survive for several months. The males are elongated after the first moult. The 3rd instar is the pre-pupal stage and the 4th instar is pupal stage. The winged adults emerge in about 1-2 months, fertilises the female and dies.

Seasonal incidence: They damage the mulberry crops throughout the year. However, the peak the incidence is observed during warmer months in hilly regions.

Nature of Damage

- They attack twigs, branches and stems, causing loss of vitality.

- Maximum damage is observed during 1.5 years of the plantation of the mulberry. It rarely attacks the older plants.
- It sucks the plant sap.
- In case of severe attack on young plant, the leaves become yellow and finally the whole plants dries up and die.
- On heavily attacks, the plant shoots are covered with reddish brown scales with dark patches of sooty mould, which grows on honeydew secreted by the insect.

Management

- Prune the infested shoots and burn them.
- Swabbing with a blunt edge wooden plate to dislodge the insect.
- Spraying of 0.05 per cent Dimethoate with a ten days safe period.
- Spraying of Lime Sulphur solution on stem.
- Swabbing of washing powder solution on the stem to dislodge the scale insect.
- Spray of 0.05 per cent Malathion with safe period of 10 days.
- Use of predators, such as the green lacewing and parasitic encirtid wasps.
- In case of severe attack, a combination of Phosmet (19 ml), Malathion (6 ml) and DDVP (4 ml) in 10 litres of water should be prepared and sprayed twice at an interval of seven days with safe period of 10 days.

(5) THRIPS *(Pseudodendrothrips mori)*

Pseudodendrothrips mori (Niwa) is commonly known as thrips or raised tail insect. It is polyphagous and a major pest of mulberry causing great concern to sericulturists all over India.

Taxonomic Position

Class	:	Insecta
Order	:	Thysanoptera
Superfamily	:	Thripoidea
Family	:	Thripiidae
Genus	:	*Pseudodendrothrips*
Species	:	*mori* (Niwa).

Status of the pest: This is a major mulberry pest and widely distributed in India, Japan, China, Sri Lanka and Vietnam. So far, 60 species have been reported on mulberry, of which about 25 are seen frequently. In India the symptoms and damage of thrips are found severe in MR2 compared to other existing mulberry varieties (Reddy and Narayanaswamy, 1999). The alternate host plant is *Ficus*. The five species of thrips commonly found in India are *Psuedodendrothrips mori, Taeniothripscalaratris, Taeniothripsglycines, Taeniothripsmelanicornis* and *Haplothripscoloratus*. They are also known as thunder flies or storm flies. Sahakundu (1994) reported population dynamics of mulberry thrips under West Bengal conditions.

Biology: After mating, the female lays 30-50 bean shaped eggs on the ventral surface of the leaf. The eggs are reniform, colourless and transparent measuring 0.02 mm in length. The incubation period ranges from 6-8 days. The nymphs are pale yellow coloured. They moult four times in 16-18 days. Nymphal stage is economically important as it causes damage to mulberry leaves. Pre-pupal and pupal stages pass in the soil. Adults exhibit sexual dimorphism, as males are smaller, brownish yellow with slender abdomen, whereas females are bigger, dark brown with broader abdomen. They reproduce both parthenogenetically and sexually. On an average adult measures 0.9 mm in length. Antennae are light yellow in colour with eight segments, of which the three segments at the end are fused and looking like a single segment. The end segment is thin and sharp and slightly dark brown in colour. Longevity of male is 10-14 days, while female survives for 15-20 days. There are generally 5-10 generations in a year. Naik (1997) detailed biocenology of thrips infesting mulberry.

Seasonal Incidence

- Thrips appear throughout the year in mulberry fields. However, the damage is very high during summer, the peak being April and May. Both nymphs and adults cause damage.
- Thrips infestation is more in rainfed mulberry gardens. Prevalence of dry weather also accelerates thrips infestation.

Nature of Damage

- Adult thrips and nymphs pierce and damage the lower surface of the leaves or petiole and cuticle with the help of piercing mouthparts and suck the sap.
- A white transparent small hollow appears on the damaged part, which loses chlorophyll and soon becomes brown. The damaged part hardens as it loses water (Das *et al.*, 1994).
- The symptoms include depletion of moisture, reduction in crude protein content and total sugars in affected leaves. The affected leaves show yellow streaks in the early stage of the attack, whereas yellow blotches are observed at advance stage of the attack, which become yellowish brown on maturity.
- Leaves become leathery and boat shaped, with deterioration in quality and the leaves fall prematurely.
- Feeding the silkworms with the infested mulberry leaves causes deterioration in the yield and quality of cocoons.
- It has been estimated that leaf yield loss due to thrips infestation is about 1300 kg/acre/season (Feb-June).
- The Economic Threshold Level (ETL) is 20 individuals per leaf.

Management: The Integrated Pest Management (IPM) of thrips includes cultural operation, chemical control and biological control.

(a) Cultural Control

- Sprinkler irrigation washes off the nymphs and adults.
- Frequent irrigation, periodical ploughing and digging of mulberry fields helps in exposing the pupae to hot sun and natural enemies and thus reducing the weed flora and in turn offers better crop (Reddy and Kotikal, 1988).
- Removal of weeds, which may serve as alternate hosts of thrips, also helps to reduce the pest population.

(b) Chemical Control

- In case of mild infestation (less than 20 thrips per plant) application of 0.1 per cent Dimethoate is recommended. In case of severe infestation, where thrips population is more than 40/leaf, 0.2 per cent application of Dimethoate is recommended twice at weekly intervals (Yey and Guz, 1990). Safe period for silkworm rearing after application of Dimethoate is 14 days.
- Rogor can be used more effectively to control thrips with a residual toxicity of 7 days.

(c) Biological Control

- Release of ladybird beetles, *Menochilus sexmaculatus* and *Scymnus coccivora, Anthocrid orius* sp. and neuropterans, which feed on thrips, can effectively control the pest population.

(6) JASSIDS *(Empoasca flavescens)*

More than 15 genera of leaf and plant hoppers are reported which causes considerable damage to mulberry plants. The major leafhoppers associated with mulberry plants are *Amrasca biguttula, Balclutha* sp., *Cicadulina bipunctata, Cofana spectra, Empoasca* sp., *Kolla ceylonica, Nephotettix nigropictus, N. vircscens* etc. The most common and widespread leafhopper is *Empoasca flavescens.* The pest commonly known as jassids has been reported as serious pest of mulberry in India. It is also known as leafhoppers or plant hoppers. Several plants like lady's finger, cotton, castor, brinjal, green and black gram, and cucurbits are the alternate host for jassids.

Taxonomic Position

Class	:	Insecta
Order	:	Hemiptera
Family	:	Cicadellidae
Genus	:	*Empoasca*
Species	:	*flavescens* (F.)

Status of the pest: It is widely reported to cause damage to mulberry in Karnataka, Tamil Nadu and Andhra Pradesh.

Biology: Female lays 20-30 pale yellow elongated eggs on the lower surface of the leaf below the epidermis. Incubation period varies from 4-7 days. There are six nymphal instars and adult stage is reached after 19-27 days. Adults are 2.5-4.0 mm in length, pale green in colour; move side ways over the edge of the leaf and fly or jump when disturbed. They are elongated tapering towards posterior end. Nymphs are similar in shape to the adults but lack the wings and are very small and pale green in colour. They usually complete their growth on the leaf where they hatch.

Seasonal incidence: The pest is prevalent during rainy/ summer months as a major pest in the country.

Nature of Damage

- The greenish adults and nymphs feeds on the under surface of the leaf sucking the sap from veins and causing characteristic symptoms known as hopper burn.

Table 2.4 : Occurrence and Life Cycle of Mulberry Sap Suckers

Name of the sap suckers	Period of occurrence	Life cycle					
		Fecundity	Hatching (days)	Nymphal period (days)	Longevity (days)		Genera-tion/ year
					Male	Female	
Mealy bug	Throughout the year. High incidence in summer	350-500	6-9	23-27 (Female-3; Male-4 instars)	3-4	10-12	15
Thrips	-do-	30-50	6-8	15-18	10-14	15-20	15
Jassid	Summer	20-30	4-7	19-27	6-9	10-15	15
Spiralling	Dec.	40-70	4-6	14-20	4-8	10-14	15
Whitefly	Prolonged dry spell followed by hot humid weather						
Scale insect	Throughout the year. High incidence in summer	500-800	5-7	19-28 (Female-4; Male 4 instars)	6-11	9-18	15

- Leaf becomes cup shaped and withers off prematurely.
- The burn is caused due to toxic virus for which the insect is a vector.
- Affected leaves are depleted in nutritive value.
- The most obvious signs of injury are the reduced stem height.
- The most prominent symptom is that the small green hoppers feed by sucking sap from leaves and cause 'hopper burn' *i.e.* yellowing of leaves all along the leaf margin.

Management

- Setting up of light traps and sticky traps for attracting and trapping adults.
- Sprinkler irrigation is effective in controlling the pest.
- Spraying of 0.1 per cent Dimethoate (Rogor) or 0.05 per cent DDVP (Nuvan), with safe period of 11 days after spray.
- Reduviid and Pentatomid predators feed on both nymphs and adults.

Occurrence and life cycle of some mulberry sap suckers is presented in Table 2.4 and sap sucking pest complex in Table 2.5.

Tolerance in Mulberry against Sap Sucking Insects

Ghosh *et al.* (2009) stated that property of resistance of plant against the pest infestation is the ability to withstand the infestation. Morphological features, physiological characteristics and biochemical constituents play an important role in making the plant resistant to pest infestation. They stated that susceptible genotype contained significantly higher levels of chlorophyll-a, chlorophyll-b, total chlorophyll, total soluble protein, total soluble sugar and leaf moisture than the tolerant genotypes. But in case of phenol content, the values in the susceptible genotype were lower than the tolerant genotype, though the difference noticed was not significant (Table 2.6).

Table 2.5 : Mulberry Sap Sucking Pest Complex

Sl. No.	Name of the pest	Order/family	Pest status	Season
1.	*Maconellicoccus hirsutus*	Homoptera: Pseudococcidae	Major	Throughout the year
2.	*Aleurodicus dispersus*	Homoptera: Aleyrodidae	Minor	March-June
3.	*Coccus viridis*	Homoptera: Coccidae	Minor	April-July
4.	*Saissetia nigra*	Homoptera: Coccidae	Minor	March-June
5.	*Pseudodentrothrips mori*	Thysanoptera: Thripidae	Major	Throughout the year
6.	*Taeniothrips melanicornis*	Thysanoptera: Thripidae	Minor	Throughout the year
7.	*Empoasca flavescens*	Homoptera: Cicadellidae	Minor	Summer
8.	*Aonidella aurentii*	Homoptera: Coccidae	Minor	Summer
9.	*Dolycoris indicus*	Heteroptera: Pentatomidae	Minor	September-January
10.	*Eusarcocoris ventralis*	Heteroptera: Pentatomidae	Occasional	September-March
11.	*Halys dentatus*	Heteroptera: Pentatomiidae	Occasional	August-March
12.	*Chrysocoris purpurea*	Heteroptera: Scutelleridae	Minor	Throughout the year
13.	*Leptocoris augur*	Heteroptera: Rhopalidae	Minor	March-June
14.	*Dysdercus cingulatus*	Heteroptera: Pyrrhocoridae	Occasional	May-June
15.	*Oxyrachis tarandus*	Homoptera: Membracidae	Minor	Throughout the year
16.	*Clovia puncta*	Homoptera: Cercopidae	Minor	July-February
17.	*Spilostethus hospus*	Heteroptera: Lygaeidae	Occasional	May-July

Source: Govindaiah *et al.,* 2005.

Table 2.6 : Biochemical and Leaf Anatomical Characteristics of Tolerant and Susceptible Genotypes

Characteristics	Tolerant genotype	Susceptible genotype	t-value (df 8)
Biochemical			
Chlorophyll-a (mg g^{-1} fresh wt.)	1.025	1.623	5.52**
Chlorophyll-b (mg g^{-1} fresh wt.)	0.378	0.635	2.69*
Total chlorophyll (mg g^{-1} fresh wt.)	1.403	2.258	8.95**
Total soluble protein (mg g^{-1} fresh wt.)	31.35	39.86	7.67**
Total soluble sugar (mg g^{-1} fresh wt.)	43.83	59.23	4.77**
Phenol content (mg g^{-1} fresh wt.)	11.97	9.63	1.77 NS
Leaf moisture content (%)	73.49	76.85	4.68**
Leaf anatomy—Thickness of different constituent layers (μ)			
Upper cuticle	14.46	5.42	15.00**
Upper epidermis	16.87	10.24	11.00**
Palisade layer	150.02	71.10	13.78**
Spongy layer	14.46	30.13	8.51**
Lower epidermis	13.26	10.85	2.45**
Lower cuticle	7.17	4.79	39.36**
Total leaf thickness	216.30	132.55	12.50**
Significant level: * 5%, ** 1%; NS- Non-significant			

Source: Ghosh *et al.*, 2009.

They further studied the anatomy of susceptible and tolerant genotypes and reported that thickness of lower cuticle and lower epidermis which acts as barrier to the sucking pests was significantly lower in the susceptible genotype. The total leaf thickness was also reported significantly higher in tolerant genotype compared to susceptible genotype. From the study they concluded that higher nutrient content of the leaves of susceptible genotype combined with lesser thickness of lower epidermis and lower cuticle may have been the possible reason, which attracted the sucking pests, on the other hand, more thickness of lower epidermis and lower cuticle in the tolerant genotype may have acted as a barrier to pest attack.

Functional Morphology and Feeding Process of Sap Sucking Insects

The functional morphology and feeding process of sap sucking insects is detailed by Rajadurai and Thiagarajan (2003). The functional mouth of the sap sucker is at the tip of the long flexible stylet bundle and arranged to reach tissues relatively far from the body of the insect. The stylet bundle is composed of paired mandibles and maxillae which have ridges and grooves. Each of the maxillae has two deep grooves opposed to form a double canal system. Saliva is pumped down the one, and fluids are sucked up through the other. The sap suckers penetrate plant tissues with the bristle like mandibular and maxillary stylets. During the natural feeding process, as the stylets are being forced into the substrate, two kinds of saliva are secreted. One becomes a gel as it discharged; it becomes a 'stylet sheath' that lines the path taken by the stylets and is eventually left behind as a 'stylet track'. Other saliva, which remains fluid, is also discharged; it is commonly termed as 'watery saliva'. During the formation of the stylet track, sheath materials as well as saliva are secreted. The sap suckers are thereby able to ingest substances from the plants and sometimes they ingest some of the sheath material before it has completed gelling.

(7) HAIRY CATERPILLAR *(Spilarctia casignata)*

Spilarctia casignata is commonly known as hairy caterpillar.

Taxonomic Position

Phylum	:	Arthropoda
Class	:	Insecta
Order	:	Lepidoptera
Family	:	Anetidae
Genus	:	*Spilarctia*
Species	:	*casignata* (Koll).

Status of pest: It is a minor pest of mulberry and is omnivorous in nature. Besides mulberry, it damages bean, cotton, maize, wheat, potato, sorghum, sunflower etc.

Biology: Eggs are laid on the under surface of the leaves and are spread evenly. They are oblate-spherical and measures 0.6 mm in diameter. Surface of eggs is reticulate. Each egg mass contains 80-200 eggs. Each moth can lay 800-1000 eggs. Larval body is cylindrical, dorsally brownish yellow, thorax with light brown sub-dorsal line and spiracles and a hairy tubercle in each segment. Larva passes through six instars in 23-42 days. Before making a cocoon, the mature larva moves in and out of the soil elongating and contracting to form a cavity, spitting threads on one side and casting off hairs on the other. The saliva and hairs intermix and form a thin cover for the cocoon. Pupa is about 18 mm long and deep brown in colour. Pupation takes place generally in soil and sometimes in stone cracks or weeds. Adult females are larger than males. There arc 5 generations in a year.

Seasonal incidence: It is a pest of mostly temperate region and affects mulberry plant in all the seasons.

Nature of Damage

- The tiny caterpillar on emerging congregate and skeletonise the under surface of leaves by feeding on the epidermal tissues. Late instars feed on whole leaves.

Management

- Timely plucking of affected leaves together with pest can effectively control pest population.
- Parasitization by natural enemy *Apanteles bosei* either during or after peak larval period reduces pest population considerably.
- Spraying of 20 times diluted kerosene emulsion or 50 times diluted pesticide soap solution exterminates the larvae.

(8) LEAF CATERPILLAR *(Margaronia pyloalis)*

It is a major pest and commonly known as mulberry pyralid.

Taxonomic Position

Phylum	:	Arthropoda
Class	:	Insecta
Order	:	Lepidoptera
Family	:	Pyralidae
Genus	:	*Margaronia*
Species	:	*pyloalis* (Walker).

Status of the pest: Widely distributed in temperate region of the country. However, it is a predominant pest throughout Kashmir valley and Jammu province. In Jammu and Kashmir, about 20-25 per cent damage to mulberry crops occurs due to this pest during July-October. Moreover, this does not affect the commercial silkworm rearing which is conducted during spring (May-June).

Biology: The female lays about 200 eggs on the margin of veins of mulberry leaves on its ventral side. The eggs are green in colour and spherical. The incubation period of eggs is 5-6 days. The egg measures about 0.7 mm in diameter, light green in colour and has flat circular shape. The caterpillar is light green at early stage whereas the mature larvae turn pink or brown. They moult 4-5 times to reach final instar. Full-grown larvae measure about 18 mm in length. The larvae hibernate in pupal stage. The pupae and adults (moths) are brown in colour. The adult moth measures about 2 cm at the wing expansion. The wing is triangular in shape and has several irregular strips of dark brown colour. The female is nocturnal laying egg within 6 hours after emergence. It completes 4 generations a year.

Seasonal incidence: The pest infestation is generally noticed in temperate region from May to October.

Nature of Damage

- The larvae defoliate the mulberry plants.
- The characteristic-feeding pattern is that the larvae webs the leaves together feeding inside and skeletonise them.
- The larvae soil the leaves with litter.

Management

- For the prevention and control of this pest, the most effective means is to use the nature of the insect to the best advantage. In other words, straw or paper should be spread over the ground around the mulberry stumps to lure mature larvae, collect and destroy by burning.
- Raking up of soil or ploughing to destroy the hibernating larvae.
- Installation of light traps to attract and collect the moths and their destruction.
- Spraying of 0.01 per cent Monocrotophos or 0.05 per cent Phasphomidon or 0.04 per cent DDVP on mulberry leaves can reduce the infestation up to 80-90 per cent (safe period 16-18 days, 18-20 days and 9 days respectively).
- The parasitoids like *Apantelis* spp. and *Chelonus* spp. can be exploited as bio-control agents against the pest.

(9) BIHAR HAIRY CATERPILLAR *(Spilosoma obliqua)*

Spilosoma obliqua commonly known as Bihar hairy caterpillar is a polyphagous pest infesting various crops including mulberry, sunflower, jute, green gram etc (Ramkishor *et al.*, 1994; Shree and Manjunath, 1998). It is voracious leaf eater causing extensive damage to mulberry (Nath *et al.*, 1994).

Taxonomic Position

Phylum	:	Arthropoda
Class	:	Insecta
Order	:	Lepidoptera
Family	:	Arctiidae
Genus	:	*Spilosoma*
Species	:	*obliqua* (Walker).

Status of the pest: The pest is reported to infest mulberry crop from many countries. This is a major pest of mulberry in southern region in India.

Biology: Female moth lay about 1000-1200 green eggs in batches. The eggs are laid on the under surface of the leaves. The eggs hatch in about 5-7 days. The newly hatched larvae are dull-white in colour with prominent black head and small dense hairs on the body. They are gregarious in habit, feed on soft tissue and leave behind the veins and veinlets of the leaves. The late age caterpillars are voracious feeders of leaves and heavily infested mulberry plant will be seen with branches without leaves. Their anterior and posterior portions are black and the middle portion is yellowish-brown in colour. The full-grown larva measures 5 cm in length. The final instar lasts for 5-7 days. The larval stage is completed in 27-31 days through 7 instars. Pupation takes place in loose soil and the pupal period is 12-14 days. Pupa is dark brown and measure 2 cm in length. The adult moths are light brown in colour, having brick-red abdomen with rows of black dots on the dorsal and lateral sides. The wings have scattered black spots.

The life cycle is completed in 40-50 days. Kotikal (1982) studied the pest biology, seasonal incidence and nature of damage in detail.

Seasonal incidence: Bihar hairy caterpillar occurs during the monsoon and post monsoon periods and the pest aestivates in pupal stage in soil during summer. Infestation is severe from August to February.

Nature of Damage

- The young larvae that hatch out, feed gregariously by scrapping the chlorophyll layers of the leaf exposing the network of veins which impart dried/ dead appearance of the leaves.
- The affected leaves look dead and dried dry and easily fall-off.
- Later instar caterpillars are voracious feeders and completely feed on leaves and tender twigs. Clear branches without leaves in the mulberry garden can also be seen after severe attack.
- Black tiny litres on lower leaves and on the ground are clear indications of the presence of the pest.

Bihar hairy caterpillar

Management

The Integrated Pest Management of Bihar hairy caterpillar includes the following aspects–

(a) Cultural Control

- Leaves containing egg masses and gregarious young instars are to be collected and destroyed at the initial stage of the pest incidence to check its multiplication in successive generations.
- Deep digging and flood irrigation for exposing and killing the pupae, which pupate in the soil, can be adopted which reduces pest population considerably.

(b) Chemical Control

- Foliar application of 0.2 per cent Dimethoate (Rogor) or 0.2 per cent DDVP (Nuvan) on mulberry plants to kill the caterpillars. Safe period for silkworm feeding of such leaves is 15-17 days after spray.
- Spray of 0.025 per cent Parathion (Folidol) on mulberry plants also kills the caterpillars. Safe period is 8 days after spray.

(c) Behavioural Control

- Installation of light traps to attract the adults of the pest, leads to subsequent reduction of the population.

(d) Biological Control

- Release *Trichogramma chilonis,* an egg parasitoid @ one tricho-card/acre/week. For effective parasitization of the host eggs in the mulberry garden, each tricho-card should be cut into 12-16 pieces and stapled at the under surface of mulberry leaf evenly. The parasitoid is able to kill 33 per cent eggs of the pest under field conditions.

- Release *Meteorus dichomeridis*, a larval parasitoid @ 1000 adults/acre/month to suppress field population of Bihar hairy caterpillar. *M. dichomeridis* parasitises through fourth stage of the pest and can kill 32 per cent of the field populations.
- Parasitoid releases have to be undertaken 20 days after pruning or harvesting.

(10) DEFOLIATOR *(Diaphania pulveruntalis)*

Diaphania pulveruntalis commonly known as defoliator is a major pest of mulberry in India.

Taxonomic Position

Phylum	:	Arthropoda
Class	:	Insecta
Order	:	Lepidoptera
Family	:	Pyralididae
Genus	:	*Diaphania*
Species	:	*pulveruntalis* (Hampson).

Status of the pest: The pest is distributed in Malaysia, Japan, Korea and India. The pest has been known to cause extensive damage to mulberry gardens in Malaysia, where several hundreds of acre of mulberry garden has been infested. In India it causes damage to mulberry crop especially in the states of Karnataka, Andhra Pradesh and Tamil Nadu as a major pest (Geethabai *et al.*, 1997; Rajadurai *et al.*, 1999). The infestation is observed in mulberry plantations from 15 days through 70 days after pruning or leaf harvest. Up to 70 per cent infestation is recorded in several areas.

Biology: Female lays 80-150 eggs, 1 or 2 eggs on the apical portion of each shoot. The eggs are flat and pink in colour and hatches in 5-7 days. After hatching the larvae moves to the apical shoot of the plant and starts feeding on the unopened leaves, resulting in drying of terminal portion of the shoot.

Grownup larvae are greenish brown with black markings on the lateral and dorsal regions of the body segments. Larval period lasts for 8-12 days. Pupation occurs in dry leaves or grass at the base of the plant. Pupae are dark brown and pupal stage lasts for 7-9 days. Adult moth emerges in early May and deposit eggs on the ventral surface of mulberry leaves. They are greyish brown and measure 1.9-2.3 cm. Life cycle is completed in 31-35 days. There are more than one generation in a year. Rajadurai *et al.* (2002a) studied the life table of leaf roller in detail.

Seasonal incidence: Though infestation is observed round the year but it attains the status of major pest during summer in the states of Karnataka and Tamil Nadu.

Nature of Damage

- The early stage larva inhibits opening of apical part of the unopened leaves. The infested leaves are brought together and bound through by silken web formed by the larva. Sometimes, single leaf is folded and completely eaten up by late age larva, resulting in considerable loss in the leaf yield.
- Grownup larvae feed voraciously on tender leaves and their faecal matter can be seen on the leaves below the affected portion.
- Occasionally, the larva also bores into the soft apical stem resulting in the drying of the shoot.
- The pest-infested plants show stunted growth (Sidde Gowda *et al.*, 1995).
- Heavily infested fields show considerable amount of webbing over the leaves. Such leaves are completely eaten up by later stage larvae resulting in considerable decline in leaf yield.
- In addition, pest larvae are also the carrier of the pebrine disease, which infect the silkworms. The larvae infected with pebrine spores in the field can contaminate mulberry leaves. When such contaminated

leaves are fed to the silkworms, it causes pebrine disease in silkworms. Thus pest causes dual damages.

Management

- Clipping and destroying of pest infested apical shoots.
- Since the pest pupates in the fallen leaves, they should be collected and burnt.
- Weeds should be removed from the mulberry plots.
- Foliar application of 0.2 per cent DDVP in 0.5 per cent soap solution (safe period is 17 days after spray for silkworm rearing). The spray solution should be applied in such a way that the apical part of the plant is properly drenched. About 200 litres of solution is required per acre of mulberry garden. Freshly prepared solutions should only be used.
- Adopt IPM strategy comprising cultural, mechanical and chemical and biological control methods for better results.
- Natural enemies on leaf roller can also be exploited as a bio-control agent (Sidde Gowda *et al.*, 1997; Rajadurai *et al.*, 2002b) (Table 2.7).

(11) CUT WORM *(Spodoptera litura)*

This is a polyphagous insect commonly known as cutworm or tobacco caterpillar. It is also known as fall armyworm or cluster caterpillar or rice cut worm. In infest several crops such as tobacco, castor and vegetable crops besides mulberry.

Taxonomic Position

Phylum	:	Arthropoda
Class	:	Insecta
Order	:	Lepidoptera
Family	:	Noctuidae
Genus	:	*Spodoptera*
Species	:	*litura* (F.)

Table 2.7: Natural Enemies of *Diaphania pulveruntalis*

Host range	Natural enemy	Order	Family
Egg	**I. Parasitoid**		
	Trichogramma chilonis	Hymenoptera	Trichogrammatidae
	II. Predator		
	Menochilus sexmaculatus	Coleoptera	Coccinellidae
Larva	**I. Parasitoid**		
	Apanteles taragamae	Hymenoptera	Braconidae
	A. machaeralis	Hymenoptera	Braconidae
	Bracon hebetor	Hymenoptera	Braconidae
	Goniosus indicus	Hymenoptera	Braconidae
	Phanerotoma hendecasisella	Hymenoptera	Braconidae
	II. Predator		
	Calasoma sp.	Coleoptera	Carabidae
	Eocanthecona furcellata	Heteroptera	Pentatomidae
	Rihirbus trocantricus	Heteroptera	Reduciidae
	Solenopsis sp.	Hymenoptera	Formicidae
	Oxyopus sp.	Arachinida	Lycosidae
Pupa	**I. Parasitoid**		
	Tetrastichus howardii	Hymenoptera	Eulophidae
	II. Predator		
	Earwigs	Dermaptera	Forficulidae

Status of the pest: *S. litura* is distributed in Asia and Australasia. In India, though polyphagous, it is considered to be one of the major pests of tobacco and hence is popularly known as tobacco caterpillar.

Biology: Eggs are laid in clusters of 200-300 underneath the leaves covered with brown hairs. Incubation period is 4-5 days. Final instar caterpillars are dark in colour and measures 50 mm in length. Larval period lasts for 2-3 weeks. The caterpillar is nocturnal in habit. The full-grown larva is stout, cylindrical and pale greenish brown in colour with dark markings. They have transverse and longitudinal grey and yellow bands. The caterpillars feed on the leaves in the nursery and in the main field and often at the young shoots and cause serious damage. Pupation occurs in the soil and pupae are dark brown in colour. Adult emerges from the pupae in about 2 weeks. The moths are stout, dark with waxy white markings on the fore wings and hind wings owe with white margins having a brown colour. The moths are attracted towards light during night. Life cycle completes in 30-40 days. There are 8 generations in a year.

Seasonal incidence: The pest infests mulberry from August to February.

Nature of Damage

- The caterpillars attack the young shoots and leaves and cut them.
- The cut portions fall down and dry up.
- Newly sprouted mulberry garden or the garden having the young plants affected by the pest is found without branches and sometimes having dried leaves.

Management

- Collection of leaves with egg masses and caterpillars and destroying them by burning.
- Deep ploughing of mulberry garden followed by flood irrigation exposes the pupal stages of pest, which can be picked-up and killed.
- Setting up of light traps attracts the adult moths and kills them.
- Spraying of 0.025 per cent Parathion (Folidol) in infested mulberry fields to kill the caterpillars. Safe period to use mulberry leaves is 8 days after spray.
- Dust 5 per cent Malathion near the base of the plants immediately after pruning or leaf harvest. Safe period to use leaf for rearing of silkworm is reported 45 days.
- Use 'Spodolure', a pheromone trap @ 2 lures/acre twice at an interval of 15 days starting from 25 days after pruning or leaf harvest to attract and kill moths.

(12) BARK CATERPILLAR *(Indarbela quadrinotata)*

Indarbela quadrinotata is commonly known as bark caterpillar or stem borer.

Taxonomic Position

Class	:	Insecta
Order	:	Lepidoptera
Family	:	Metarbelidae
Genus	:	*Indarbela*
Species	:	*quadrinotata* (Walker).

Status of the pest: It is an occasional pest on mulberry in the states of Karnataka, Andhra Pradesh and Tamil Nadu. It is polyphagous on most trees and woody shrubs.

Biology: The female lays as many as 2000 eggs in clusters of 18-25 eggs. The incubation period is 8-10 days. The newly hatched larvae are dirty brown while the full-grown caterpillars are pale brown and measures 50-60 mm in length. The larvae have the habit of making webs along the feeding galleries and above the holes. The larvae complete development in 9-11 months. They pupate in hole in the wood. Pupal period lasts for 3-4 weeks. The adults are pale brown moths with rufous head and thorax. The fore wings are pale rufous with numerous dark rufous bands. Their hind wings are fuscous. The moths emerge and become active with the start of summer season. Only one generation is completed in a year.

Seasonal incidence: It is a serious pest of tree mulberry and causes damage to the bark. Its infestation starts with the onset of monsoon. The rate of infestation is influenced by rainfall and other associated factors.

Nature of Damage

- Larvae have the habit of making webs. Only one larva is seen inside a hole, which is used, only as a shelter when it does not feed during daytime.

- They eat through the bark in the wood and in case of severe infestation, sap movement is interfered and trees cease to flush and the growth is arrested.

Management

- Insert into the boreholes insecticides soaked cotton plugs and plaster on the outside with mud during February-March.
- Spraying of 0.01 per cent Monocrotophos (36% EC) on the tree trunk area avoiding foliage.

(13) RED HAIRY CATERPILLAR *(Amsacta albistringa)*

Amsacta albistringa is polyphagous pest and is commonly known as red hairy caterpillar.

Taxonomic Position

Class	:	Insecta
Order	:	Lepidoptera
Family	:	Arctiidae
Genus	:	*Amsacta*
Species	:	*albistringa* (Walker).

Status of the pest: It is a minor pest widely distributed in mulberry growing areas in India in general and Karnataka, Tamil Nadu and Andhra Pradesh in particular.

Biology: Female lays 700-1000 eggs on the under surface of the leaves of mulberry plants. The eggs are light yellow in colour and spherical in shape. The incubation period is 2-3 days. There are 6 larval stages and larval period varies from 15-25 days. The larvae enter the soil, shed their hairs and make thin cocoons at a depth of about 10-15 cm. The colour of full-grown caterpillar varies from reddish amber to olive green and body is covered with numerous long hairs arising from the fleshy tubercles. They measure about 25 mm in length. The adults are medium sized moths. The fore wings are white with brown streaks all over and yellowish streak along the anterior margin and the hind wings white with black spots. A yellow band is seen on the head. The insect undergoes pupal diapause in the soil and becomes active from June to August.

Nature of Damage

- The young caterpillars feed gregariously and as they grow older they march in bands destroying field after field of mulberry plants.

Management

- Light traps should be put-up at night following showers of monsoon.
- Deep ploughing should be followed during summer.
- 0.5 per cent Endosulfan 35 EC, 200 ml of Dichlorovos 100 EC in 100-200 litres of water per acre may be sprayed for control of the pest.

(14) MORINGA HAIRY CATERPILLAR *(Eupterote mollifera)*

Eupterote mollifera is commonly known as Moringa hairy caterpillar.

Taxonomic Position

Class	:	Insecta
Order	:	Lepidoptera
Family	:	Eupterotidae
Genus	:	*Eupterote*
Species	:	*mollifera* (Walker).

Status of the pest: It is a minor pest causing damage to mulberry crop in the entire mulberry growing areas of India.

Biology: Freshly laid eggs are sulphur yellow in colour, which later change into brownish yellow. Eggs laid are attached to the tender twigs or on to the petiole of leaves. Eggs are round in shape, slightly flattened at the top with a small depression. Incubation period is 9-13 days. Larvae usually moult four times in approximately 68 days to pass through the five instars. Final stage caterpillars are dark in colour with thick coat of hairy tufts and each measure 48-50 mm in length. Pupation takes place in soft thin cocoon made of silk secreted along with the hairs of the caterpillars under the leaves. Pupa is dark brown in colour. It measures 18-20 mm in length. Pupal stage lasts for 35-60 days. Male moths are smaller in size and light yellow in colour. Females are larger and dark brown in colour. Pillai (1968 a & c) detailed the bionomics of the pest.

Seasonal incidence: Incidence of pest is generally high during August-February.

Nature of Damage

- Larvae feed on mulberry leaves and thereby causing reduction in leaf yield.
- Mulberry plants with only branches and without leaves are seen in the field affected with the pest.

Management

- Collection of leaves with egg masses, caterpillars and burning them.
- Deep digging exposes pupae to their predators.
- Flood irrigation suffocates them to death.
- Light traps attract the adult moths and kill them.
- Spraying of 0.025 per cent Parathion (Folidol) in infested mulberry fields (Safe period: 8 days).

(15) TUSSOCK CATERPILLAR *(Euproctis fraterna)*

Euproctis fraterna commonly known as Tussock caterpillar of mulberry. In addition to mulberry, it also damages peach, apple, cherry, pear etc.

Taxonomic Position

Class : Insecta
Order : Lepidoptera
Family : Lymantridae
Genus : *Euproctis*
Species : *fraterna* (Moore).

Status of the pest: The pest causes damage to mulberry crops during summer especially in the states of Karnataka, Andhra Pradesh and Tamil Nadu.

Biology: Within 12-14 hrs of mating female moth lays 100-120 pale yellow coloured oval eggs in masses covered with yellow hairs on the underside of mulberry leaves. The incubation period is 15-18 days. The hatched larvae are yellow in colour with dark tufts of hairs on the 2nd and 3rd abdominal segments. They feed on mulberry leaves gregariously. The final instar caterpillars are dark brown in colour and measure 35-40 mm in length. Larvae moults four times and total larval duration is approximately 60 days. The last instar larvae make loose silk cocoons in the plant debris lying on the ground and pupate inside. Pupal stage lasts about 13-15 days. Moths are yellow in colour. Initially male emergence is higher than female, later the ratio of male: female emergence becomes 1: 1, signifying the peak period. During day the moths hide in dark crevices. Two dark spots are present on the apical angle and two larger ones on the cubital angle of the forewings of the female. Male has an additional dark spot near the coastal margin of the forewings. Mating of moths takes place within 24-28 hrs after emergence. The average longevity of male is 8-9 days and that of the female is 9-10 days. The pest completes several generations in a year.

Seasonal incidence: Incidence mostly occurs from March to August.

Nature of Damage

- Caterpillars feed on mulberry leaves.

- Branches of mulberry plants without leaves are observed in the fields affected with this pest.
- The damaged plants remain stunted and there is a considerable reduction in foliage production.

Management

- Collection of leaves with egg masses, caterpillars and burning them.
- Deep digging followed by flood irrigation exposes the pupal stages and kill them.
- Setting up of light traps attracts the adult moths and kills them.
- Spraying of 0.025 per cent Parathion (Folidol) in infested mulberry fields (safe period: 8 days).
- Dusting of 5 per cent Aldrin @ 10 kg/acre.
- Since, the caterpillar attacks several varieties of trees; those in the vicinity of sericulture farm should be treated chemically.

(16) LOOPER *(Hyposidra talaca)*

Hyposidra talaca commonly known as looper of mulberry.

Taxonomic Position

Class : Insecta

Order : Lepidoptera

Family : Geometridae

Genus : *Hyposidra*

Species : *talaca* (Walker).

Status of the pest: Minor pest affecting mulberry crop throughout the year.

Biology: Female lays about 2000 eggs in crevices in the bark. The eggs are pale blue or green and oval measuring

0.70 mm in length. Larva moults five times and larval period lasts for 25-42 days. Full-grown larvae are 5 mm in length. Pupation takes place in soil. A pupa is 18-20 mm in length and pupal period lasts 14-21 days. Wing colour in adult is variable but generally grey with many dark grey markings. The adult survives for 14 days and then dies.

Seasonal incidence: The pest causes damage to mulberry crop in summer and rainy seasons throughout the country.

Nature of Damage

- Larvae are defoliator and branches of mulberry plants are noticed without leaves.
- Pest attack leads to reduction in leaf yield.

Management

- Light trap monitoring and collection of adults.
- Summer ploughing to expose pupae to predatory birds.
- Spraying of 0.05 per cent Malathion (safe period: 10 days).

Mulberry leaf eating pest complex is summarized and presented in Table 2.8.

(17) MULBERRY WEEVIL

The weevil group of insects is widely distributed and polyphagous in nature infesting a number of agricultural and horticultural crops as plantation and tuber crops. All these days, the weevils since did not cause visible damage, were considered as minor pets and hence received no attention. However, relatively recently, severe infestation of weevils in potential sericultural areas have been reported and calls for urgent measures to control the pest, before it attains the status of major pest.

(i) Episomus fungulus: *Episomus* is commonly known as mulberry weevil.

Table 2.8 : Mulberry Leaf Eating Pest Complex

S.No.	Name of the leaf eater	Common name	Order	Family	Pest status	Season
1.	*Diaphania pulverulentalis*	Leaf roller	Lepidoptera	Pyralidae	Major	June-February
2.	*Spilarctia obliqua*	Bihar hairy caterpillar	Lepidoptera	Arctidae	Sporadic	August-February
3.	*Spodoptera litura*	Cur worm	Lepidoptera	Noctuidae	Minor	September-February
4.	*Eupterote mollifera*	Moringa hairy caterpillar	Lepidoptera	Eupterotidae	Minor	September-February
5.	*Euproctis fraternal*	Tussock caterpillar	Lepidoptera	Lymantridae	Minor	February-June
6.	*Amata passalis*	Wasp moth	Lepidoptera	Amatidae	Minor	February-June
7.	*Ceryx godarti*	Amatid moth	Lepidoptera	Amatidae	Minor	February-June
8.	*Trichoplusia sp.*	Semi-looper	Lepidoptera	Geometridae	Minor	July-December
9.	*Archips micaceana*	Leaf tier	Lepidoptera	Tortricidae	Minor	June-March
10.	*Paradoxecia pieli*	Clear winged moth	Lepidoptera	Aegeriidae	Minor	August-November
11.	*Amieta sp.*	Bagworm	Lepidoptera	Psychidae	Minor	May-February

S.No.	Name of the leaf eater	Common name	Order	Family	Pest status	Season
12.	*Rondotria menciana*	White caterpillar	Lepidoptera	Bombycidae	Minor	September-December
13.	*Amssacta mori*	Black hairy caterpillar	Lepidoptera	Arctidae	Minor	August-December
14.	*Myllocerus subfasciatus*	Mulberry weevil	Coleoptera	Curculionidae	Minor	Throughout the year
15.	*Myllocerus viridanus*	Weevil	Coleoptera	Curculionidae	Minor	Throughout the year
16.	*Holotrichia serrata*	Cockchafer beetle	Coleoptera	Melolonthidae	Minor	April-June
17.	*Neorthacris acuticeps niligriensis*	Wingless grasshopper	Orthoptera	Acrididae	Minor	Throughout the year
18.	*Cyrtacantha-cris ranacea*	Grasshopper	Orthoptera	Acrididae	Minor	February-July

Source: Govindaiah *et al*., 2005.

Taxonomic Position

Class	:	Insecta
Order	:	Coleoptera
Family	:	Cerambycidae
Genus	:	*Episomus*
Species	:	*fungulus.*

Status of the pest: It is an occasional pest found damaging mulberry crops throughout the country.

..iology: Female lays 150-350 eggs in superficial layer of the soil over a period of 20-90 days. There are four instars of grubs after which they pupate in the soil. The adults are brownish in colour. Rostrum is long, big and curved somewhat towards inside. The head is prolonged into a snout, which varies considerably in size, shape and length. They complete 3-5 generations in a year.

Seasonal incidence: The pest is found throughout the year but maximum damage is observed during July-October.

Nature of Damage

- Both adult and grubs cause injury to mulberry.
- The weevil eats young buds or young leaves. In this process mulberry trees are seriously injured.
- The grubs feed on the underground parts of the mulberry.
- In case of severe attack the plants wilt and dry up.
- Irregular serrated margins on foliage are observed which the feeding grubs cause.

Management

- Digging of the soil up to a depth of 7-8 cm and destruction of the eggs, grubs and pupae.
- Spraying of 0.01 per cent Quinalphos (safe period: 7 days) or 0.02 per cent Methyl parathion (safe period: 10 days) or Malathion (safe period: 8 days).

(ii) Myllocerus discolor: *Myllocerus* commonly known as weevil is reported from India and Bangladesh.

Taxonomic Position

Class	:	Insecta
Order	:	Coleoptera
Family	:	Curculionidae
Genus	:	*Myllocerus*
Species	:	*discolor* (Boheman).

Status of the pest: It is an occasional pest found damaging mulberry crops throughout the country.

Biology: Female lays 150-350 eggs over a period of 20-90 days in superficial layer of the soil. The grubs hatch out from the eggs in 4-8 days. There are four instars of grubs after which they pupate inside the soil. The adults are grey and black coloured measuring 0.5-1.5 cm in length. The head is more or less prolonged into a snout, which varies considerably in size, shape and length. They complete normally 3-5 generations in a year.

Seasonal incidence: The pest is prevalent during summer season. However, their presence is noticed throughout the year.

Nature of Damage

- Both adult and grubs cause injury to mulberry.
- The adult feed on the young leaves and young buds whereas grubs feed on the underground parts of the mulberry.
- In case of severe attack the plants wilt and dry up.
- Irregular serrated margins on foliage are observed which the feeding grubs cause.

Management

- Digging or ploughing of the soil up to a depth of 7-8 cm deep and exposing the eggs, grubs and pupae to sunlight/natural enemies like birds and other predators.

- Flood irrigating the mulberry garden after digging and soil exposure so that the grubs and pupae are killed.
- Exposing the soil root zone and dusting of BHC powder also reduces infestation of the pest.
- Spraying of 0.01 per cent Quinalphos (safe period: 7 days) or 0.02 per cent Methyl Parathion (safe period: 10 days) or Malathion (safe period: 8 days).
- The pest being polyphagous in nature, control measures in adjoining crops should also be taken up simultaneously for effective management of weevils.

(18) LONGHORN BEETLE *(Batocera rufomaculata)*

Batocera rufomaculata commonly known as longhorn beetle is a major pest of mulberry.

Taxonomic Position

Class	:	Insecta
Order	:	Coleoptera
Family	:	Cerambycidae
Genus	:	*Batocera*
Species	:	*rufomaculata* (De Geer).

Status of the pest: It is a major pest of mulberry plants in temperate region of India. It is widely distributed in Darjeeling, Kumaon hills, Kullu valley, Jammu & Kashmir, Doon valley and Shimla hills.

Biology: Female lays 50-60 eggs. The eggs are oval in shape and brown in colour and laid singly in the bark of mulberry. The eggs hatch in 8-15 days. The grubs first feed on the bark and then bore inside the wood. The grubs are pale yellow and measure 90-150 mm in length. Pre-pupal stage lasts 50-70 days and pupal stage 50-75 days. The beetles are greenish brown with white lateral band all along the length of body. There are two orange-yellow spot on pronotum, numerous yellow spots on elytra and yellow or green colour on scutellum. They complete their development inside the stem. The beetles emerge in June-July and live for 4-5 months. During this period, they mate and lay eggs.

Seasonal incidence: It occurrence is mostly observed in temperate region from December to March.

Nature of Damage

- The young grubs feed on the inner side of the bark making zigzag tunnels. Later on, the grubs bore down to the surface of the sapwood and up to the centre of the heartwood.
- In case of severe infestation, the plants may die.

Management

- Grubs and adults should be mechanically destroyed.
- Plugging the holes with cotton soaked in kerosene, petroleum or Monochrotophos 0.05 per cent.

(19) LEAF BEETLE *(Mimastra cyanura)*

Mimastra cyanura is commonly known as leaf beetle or almond beetle. It is polyphagous in nature affecting a wild range of forest trees as also domesticated fruit plants which includes almonds, fig, wild pear, apricot etc (Mukharjee *et al.*, 1995).

Taxonomic Position

Class	:	Insecta
Order	:	Coleoptera
Family	:	Chrysomelidae
Genus	:	*Mimastra*
Species	:	*cyanura* (Hope)

Status of the pest: It is an occasional pest and found damaging mulberry crops throughout the country especially during rainy season.

Biology: Adults are small (8-10 mm) with prominent antennae; elytra dull yellow with bluish posterior end. Abdomen black vertically. Antennae are 11 segmented and filiform. They attack mulberry plantation in large groups and completely defoliate the plants leaving only the shoot. Tender shoots are also eaten occasionally. There are one or sometimes two generations in a year. The eggs are laid in soil. They are global, wheat-stalk—yellow with a diameter of 0.7 - 1.0 mm. The larvae (grub) are cylindrical, slightly flat and curved. Fully-grown larva is 10 mm in length with black head, thorax and thoracic legs. Abdomen is earth-yellow in colour. Pupa is about 8-9 mm in length with yellowish colour. They feed heavily in the evening and early morning hours. On cloudy days, beetles remain active throughout the day. The beetles are not the active fliers and upon shaking of the tree, they often drop down.

Seasonal incidence: They attack mulberry plantation especially during rainy season.

Nature of Damage

- Beetles eat up all the leaves including veins and midribs. With a slight disturbance, the beetle flies away from one plant to another.
- Adult beetles appear in large groups and feed voraciously on tender, medium and coarse mulberry leaves and then move to another mulberry plant.

Management

- Use light traps for collection and destruction of adults.
- Deep ploughing of soil to expose grubs.
- Soil application of Fensulfothion 5 per cent G @ 30-40 kg/ha.
- Spraying of 0.25 per cent Matacid.

(20) CHAFER GRUBS *(Schizonycha ruficallis)*

Schizonycha ruficallis is commonly known as Chafer grubs.

Taxonomic Position

Class : Insecta
Order : Coleoptera
Family : Scarabaeidae
Genus : *Schizonicha*
Species : *ruficallis* (Fab.).

Status of the pest: It is a minor pest in temperate region.

Biology: Eggs are laid in soil, especially where there is high organic content. The larvae are white, fleshy with swollen abdomen and well-developed thoracic legs. The larval stage lasts for 5-6 months. Adults are medium sized and golden brown in colour with swollen abdomen posteriorly. They are nocturnal.

Seasonal incidence: The pest causes considerable damage during summer and rainy season.

Nature of Damage

- Adult defoliates young mulberry plants.

Management

- Collection and destruction of adults using light traps.
- Deep ploughing of soil to expose grubs to natural enemies.
- Soil application of Fensulphothion 5 per cent @ 30-40 kg/hac.

(21) TERMITES *(Odontotermus obsesus)*

Termites are commonly known as white ants. Various species of termites are reported to occasionally cause damage to mulberry. The major ones are *O. obsesus, O. wallonensis, O. redemani, O. horni, Microtermes obesi, Microcentrotermes* spp. etc.

Taxonomic Position

Class	:	Insecta
Order	:	Isoptera
Family	:	Termitidae
Genus	:	*Odontotermus*
Species	:	*obsesus* (Rambur).

Status of the pest: Termites are social insects. Though they are found in all types of soils but are more frequent in the sandy and red loamy soils. It causes considerable damage to mulberry crop during summer season.

Biology: The termites or white ants are polyphagous, photophobic soil dwelling insects. They live in colonies. Each colony consists of workers (wingless, dark headed and possess strong mouth parts), soldiers (wingless, with stronger mandibles), alate (winged forms, considered as males of the colony) and a queen (winged form, with enlarged white coloured abdomen that consists of thousands of ovarioles). Wings are present only in the sexually matured males and females. During the swarming season wings of these sexually matured members fall-off following a shorter flight. The individuals separate in pairs and a cell is excavated in the soil or wood where the mating usually takes place. The eggs are deposited normally singly. Mature queen is a phenomenal egg-laying machine ovipositing one egg per second or 70,000 - 80,000 eggs in 24 hrs. Incubation period varies from 24-90 days. Duration of development and number of nymphal instars vary greatly with the form of casts and the prevailing environmental factors. Workers of the colony cause the major damage. Within 6 weeks, larvae develop to form soldiers or workers. The reproductive castes mature in 1-2 years. There is only one queen in a colony and normally she lives from 5-10 years, sometimes extending up to 20 years. The queen is fed by the workers and is always confined to the royal chamber with male (king) and form the sole function of reproduction. The male's life is much shorter than that of the queen and when he dies, a new one replaces him. The workers develop from fertilized eggs but remain stunted as they are reared on ordinary food. Except for the reproduction and defence of the community, the workers perform all other duties. The soldiers develop from unfertilised eggs and remain comparatively underdeveloped. Soldiers defend the colony mainly against other insects like ants and predators.

Seasonal incidence: The termite infestations to mulberry starts when the rain recede, usually from October onwards and continues till the onset of monsoon rains.

Nature of damage: Based on the nature of damage, termite infestation has been classified into three categories:

- Termites infesting cuttings in the nursery and new plantations – Termites attack the cuttings below the ground. They feed on the bark as well as hard wood. As a result, the cuttings dry up and do not sprout. The attack is severe in red sandy loam soils.
- Termite infesting dried twigs and plants in old plantations – In this case, termite first attack the old dried twigs. Later, they attack the live twigs and enter the hard wood of main stem and twigs. The foraging galleries are formed inside the main stem and extend below the ground. The infested twigs dry up.
- Termite infesting the pruned plants – Termites form sheathing at the tip of the pruned mulberry twigs and feed on them. This act of covering and feeding hinders the sprouting of new shoots.

Management

- Location and destruction of termite colonies by breaking the mound and killing the queen. The mound destruction can be taken up during rainy season when it is easy to dig open the mounds.
- Removal of rooting, dead, dried twigs and leaves from the garden.

- Flood irrigation kills all the stages of colony and helps to reduce the termite attack.
- Application of two tablets of Aluminium phosphide or Phorate 10 G @ 50 gm/100 sq ft of soil (safe period: 15 days).
- Application of 0.1 per cent Dursban (Chloropyriphos) (safe period: 15 days).
- Treatment of mulberry cuttings in 0.1 per cent Chloropyri-phos solution before planting.
- Soil treatment with Heptachlor 6 per cent dust, Aldrin 2.5 per cent dust or Chlordane 5 per cent dust @ 20-25 kg/ha may be followed for pre-established garden.
- In case of established garden, swabbing or drenching at the base with 0.5-1 per cent Chlordane may be followed (safe period: 20-25 days).
- There is symbiotic relationship between fungi and termites as the latter do not survive without fungi (Gowda *et al.*, 1995). Termite can be controlled by destroying the fungi *Termitomyces* sp. or by depressing the activity of fungal growth in the nests. This can be achieved by treating the mounds with fungicides like Captan (75 SD), Captafol (80 WP) or Carboxin (95 WP) @ 30 gm diluted in 15 litres of water per mound.
- Use entomopathogenic fungi and plant extracts for termite control.
- Make heap around the base of plant of wood ash or a mixture of cow dung and aloe.

(22) STEM GIRDLER BEETLE *(Sthenias grisator)*

Sthenias grisator is commonly known as stem girdler beetle.

Taxonomic Position

Class	:	Insecta
Order	:	Coleoptera

Family : Cerambycidae

Genus : *Sthenias*

Species : *grisator* (Fab.)

Status of the pest: It has been reported to damage mulberry plants both in tropical and temperate regions of India. Besides mulberry, it also attacks Casuarina, mango, jack and croton etc.

Biology: Female lays eggs beneath the bark of the girdled branches of mulberry at night. The incubation period is approximately 6-8 days. The grub tunnels into the wilting branches and feed. Grubs pupate inside the tunnel. The adults are stoutly built longicorn grey coloured beetles with rough surface, long antennae and strongly developed mouthparts. The life cycle is completed in about 7-8 months.

Seasonal incidence: The occurrence of the pest is recorded throughout the year.

Nature of Damage

- The beetles girdle the young or green branches of mulberry plants.
- The grub tunnels into the wilting branches and feeds. The branches dry and die.
- They eat away the cortical portion of the roots under the soil.
- Girdled branches of the plant or wilting plants are the main symptoms of the pest infestation.

Management

- Deep ploughing and flood irrigation are effective in controlling the grubs.
- Cutting and burning of the effected branches and stems.
- Spraying of the base of main stem or branches with 0.1 per cent BHC (safe period: 11 days) or 0.1 per cent Malathion emulsion (safe period: 11 days).

- Aldrin at the rate of 12 kg/acre is effective in minimising the grub population (safe period: 15 days).

(23) STEM BORER *(Apriona germarii)*

Apriona germarii is commonly known as stem borer beetle.

Taxonomic Position

Class	:	Insecta
Order	:	Coleoptera
Family	:	Cerambycidae
Genus	:	*Apriona*
Species	:	*germarii* (Hope).

Status of the pest: Pest attack is noticed throughout the year in various parts of the country. However, it causes severe damage of mulberry crop in Jammu region.

Biology: Female lays eggs on the trunk of branches usually in crevices of the bark. Egg hatching takes place between 7-10 days of oviposition and grub starts burrowing under the bark in the sapwood. The adults are dark grey beetles measuring about 4-6 mm in length. Males are smaller with longer antennae than females. They mate on the trunks few days after emergence. The life span varies 1-2 years mostly depending on climatic conditions. Pupation takes place inside the tunnel. Severely damaged plants may die. Frass expulsion holes are made at intervals along the main gallery, hence frass is seen externally and these provide conspicuous symptom of attack.

Seasonal incidence: The pest is found damaging the mulberry crop throughout the year in different parts of the country.

Nature of Damage

- Twigs are easily broken by winds because the tissues are partially damaged by the adults during egg laying process.

- Grubs tunnel along the branches in the tree trunk just under the bark or in the wood.
- Severely attacked plants may die.

Management

- Cutting and burning of heavily infested shoots and branches.
- In case of main stems, insert cotton soaked in good fumigants like carbon bisulphide and chloroform in the holes and seal them with mud. Besides, injecting kerosene oil, creosote, crude oil or petrol into holes has also been reported to give satisfactory results).
- Metasystox (@ 5 ml/bore) and EDB (Ethylene Dibromide) ampoules (3 ml/bore) can totally eliminate the pest without any phytotoxin effect on mulberry (Sharma and Tara, 1985).
- Injection of a mixture of 0.1 per cent Monocrotophos and kerosene 1 : 1 into the frass holes to kill the boring larvae.

(24) LONG-TAILED MEALYBUG *(Pseudococcus longispinus)*

Taxonomic Position

Phylum	:	Arthropoda
Class	:	Insecta
Order	:	Homoptera
Family	:	Pseudococcidae
Genus	:	*Pseudococcus*
Species	:	*longispinus* (Targioni-Tozzetti)

Status of the pest: The pest is wide spread throughout the world. It is minor pest of mulberry causes damage in southern part of the country. Its occurrence was first reported from Tamil Nadu during 2011.

Alternate hosts: Long-tailed mealybug has a wide host range and infests many cultivated plants including guava, coconut, citrus, mango, pigeon pea, potato, sugarcane etc.

Biology: Adult female is wingless, oval in shape, measures 3.00 mm long with short antennae and legs, has 17 pairs of waxy filaments around the periphery. Adult male is tiny (1.00 mm long) with one pair of transparent wings and long antennae. They complete 4-6 generations in a year. They do not produce egg sac and eggs hatch as soon as they are laid, giving the impressions that the young are born rather than hatching from eggs (ovoviviparous). About 100-240 eggs are laid per female. Soon after beginning to feed, they exude a white waxy covering over the body giving them a mealy appearance. After first moult, male and female are differentiated. Sexual reproduction is obligatory. The adult male survives only for 2-3 days, while the female takes 2-3 weeks maturing her eggs and up to two months to lay them. However, more than 90 per cent eggs are laid within first 10-14 days.

Nature of Damage

- Both nymphs and adults suck the sap of the plant.

Long-tailed mealybug

- Infestation hampers the vigour the growth of the plants and reduces the yield and quality of mulberry leaves.
- The symptoms appear in the leaves as chlorosis (yellowing), deformation of leaves and premature drop followed by stunted growth of the plants.

Management

- Planting of highly susceptible host plants such as guava, hibiscus, crotons etc. around the mulberry garden should be avoided.
- Cutting of the infested twigs and leaves and burning off during early stage of infestation.
- Release of *Cryptolaemus montrouzieri* an effective mealy bud destroyer can keep the peat population suppressed.
- Spray of dimethoate (0.05%) controls the pest effectively. Safe period 15 days after spraying the insecticide.

(25) PAPAYA MEALYBUG *(Paracoccus marginatus)*

Taxonomic Position

Phylum : Arthropoda

Class : Insecta

Order : Hemiptera

Family : Pseudococcidae

Genus : *Paracoccus*

Species : *marginatus* (Williams & Willink).

Status of the pest: Minor pest of mulberry reported for the first time causing damage to mulberry plantation from Tamil Nadu during January 2009.

Alternate hosts: It has been recorded on more than 55 host plants in more than 25 genera. Important host plants of the pest are papaya, hibiscus, citrus, cotton, tomato, beans, peas, mango, cherry etc.

Biology: The adult female is yellow and is covered with white waxy coating. Adult females are approximately 2.2 mm long and 1.4 mm wide. Eggs are greenish yellow and are laid in an egg sac. The adult males are coloured pink and are approximately 1.0 mm long, with an elongate oval body. Female have no wings and move by crawling short distances or being blown in air currents. Female usually lay 100-600 eggs in an ovisac. Egg laying usually occurs over a period of one to two weeks. Egg hatches in about 10 days and nymphs or crawlers begin to actively search for feeding sites. Female crawlers have four instars and take approximately one month to complete the life cycle. Males have five instars. The fifth instar of the male is the only winged form of the species capable of flight. Adult females attract the males with sex pheromones.

Nature of Damage

- Feeds on the sap of the plant resulting in chlorosis, plant stunting, leaf deformation, early leaf fall, heavy build-up of honeydew.

Management

- Burn the entire garden and burn the infested shoots.
- After pruning spray 0.2 per cent DDVP over the pruned shoots and soil around the stump.
- Second spray of 0.1 per cent Rogor 30 EC is given, 10 days after pruning.
- Third spray of 0.2 per cent DDVP or neem formulation @ ml/10 lit, mixed in 0.5 per cent soap oil solution may be given 10 days after second spray.
- One week after 3rd spray, predatory ladybird beetle (*Cryptolaemus montrouzieri*) @ 250 beetles/acre may be released.

(26) GRASSHOPPERS *(Neorthacris acuticeps nilgriensis)*

More than ten species of shorthorn grasshoppers causing damage to mulberry are reported from Karnataka (Narayanaswamy and Ramegowda, 1999) (Table 2.9). *Neorthacris acuticeps nilgriensis* is most abundant wingless shorthorn grasshopper species.

Taxonomic Position

Class : Insecta

Order : Orthoptera

Family : Acrididae

Genus : *Neorthacris*

Species : *acuticeps nilgriensis* (Uvarov).

Status of the pest: The pest causes considerable damage to rain-fed mulberry plantation grown in black cotton soils in South India.

Biology: Female lays 6-8 egg pods (ootheca), each with 11-18 eggs. Egg pods are deposited in loose soil at a depth of 2-3 cm. Incubation period of the eggs is 28-31 days. Nymphs pass through 6 moults and become adults. Early instar nymphs are light brown in colour whereas later instar nymphs and adults are green in colour. Nymphal period is 90-95 days. Adults do not have wings. Females are larger than males and live for 45-60 days. It completes its life cycle in 5-6 months.

Seasonal incidence: Throughout the year but pest status is achieved during July-August. Branches of plants without leaves are observed in the mulberry field.

Nature of Damage

- Nymphs as well as adults voraciously feed on sprouting buds and mulberry leaves causing considerable reduction in yield.
- They also feed on green bark.

- When the infestation is severe, mulberry plants are completely devoid of leaves and mulberry twigs will be visible.

Grasshopper

Management

- Exposing egg masses by deep ploughing after onset of monsoon to expose the ootheca for destruction by natural enemies.
- Spraying of 0.2 per cent DDVP (2.63 ml in one litre of water) to mulberry garden and surroundings, if the pest infestation is severe. For one acre of mulberry plantation, approximately 400 litres of solution will be required for single spray.

- Safe period for using the mulberry leaves for feeding to the silkworms is 15 days after treatment.
- Maintain field sanitation by keeping the mulberry garden free from alternate host plants of the pest.

Table 2.9 : Grasshoppers on Mulberry

S. N.	Family / Species	Period of occurrence
	Family: Acrididae	
1	*Colemanis spheneriodea*	July-October
2	*Cyrtocanthacris tatarica*	April-October
3	*Diabolocatantops pinguis innotabilis*	June-September
4	*Eucoptacra praemorsa*	June-September
5	*Heteropternis respondens*	June-September
6	*Neorthacris acuticeps niligiransis*	January-December
7	*Oxya fuscovittata*	January-October
8	*Oxya fuscovittata*	January-September
9	*Spathostemum prasinifernum prasinifernum*	September-February
	Family: Pyrgomorphidae	
10	*Atractomorpha crenulata crenulata*	January-October
	Family: Tettigonidae	
11	*Pheneroptera gracilis*	February-November
12	*Latarna inflate*	August-December
13	*Aiolopus simulatrix simulatrix*	December-February

(27) MITES *(Tetranychus telarius)*

As many as 15 species of mites have been reported to infest mulberry causing injury to the crop (Pillai and Jolly, 1980; Banerjee, 1988; Narayanaswamy *et al.*, 1996). They are characterized by having four pairs of legs in the adult stage. Some other species are *T. kanzawai, T. cinnabarinus, Panonychus eiri, Eotetranychus siginanamensis, Polyphagotarsonemus latus etc.*

Taxonomic Position

Class	:	Arachnida
Order	:	Acarina
Family	:	Tetranychidae
Genus	:	*Tetranychus*
Species	:	*telarius* (L.)

Status of the pest: It is an occasional pest causing damage to mulberry crop throughout the country.

Biology: Female lays 60-80 spherical eggs. The eggs are red, very minute and spherical in shape usually attached on the under surface of the leaves. The incubation period is 2-6 days. Young ones are pink in colour. The life cycle of mites consists of six legged larval phase followed by two nymphal stages with four pairs of legs and the adult stage also with four pairs of legs. In between the nymphal stages is the inactive resting or quiescent stages. *T. telarius* is red, green or orange in colour. The males are slightly smaller. Adult longevity is 7-12 days. Female moults thrice, while the male only once. The duration of the life cycle varies from species to species depending on the climatic conditions (Banerjee, 1988). Usually one generation is completed within 18 - 40 days, though overlapping generations are also very common .The damage is caused both by nymphs and adults.

Seasonal incidence: Generally mite infestation is stray and sporadic during drier months. The infestation is common during December to May. During summer the mites may attain pest status.

Nature of Damage

- The nymphs and adults feed together on the lower sides of the leaves between the main veins, which appear as yellow spots.
- In severe cases of infestation, leaves lose their green healthy colour and become rusty, gradually dry and fall-off resulting in the reduction of leaf yield.

- Infested plants are often covered with extensive fine webbing.
- The mites feed through sucking mouthparts with which it pierces the leaf epidermis.
- The under surface of infested leaves shows silken thread spun across them under which the mites crawl and also lay eggs.

Management

- Sprinkler irrigation disperses the life stages and hence reduces the pest incidence.
- Pruning of affected parts and branches and their destruction preferably by burning.
- Spray of 0.05-0.1 per cent Zolone, 0.1 per cent Sulfex or 0.04 per cent Dicofol. Allow safe period of 2 weeks before feeding the leaves to the worms.
- Different species of predatory coccinellids, staphylinds, cecidomyiids and chrysopids have proven to be efficient natural enemies in suppressing pest population of mites.

YELLOW MITE *(Polyphagotarsonemus latus)*: Tarsonemid mite infestation often confuses with those of nutrient deficient leaf, as the mite is not easily detectable due to microscopic size.

Taxonomic Position

Class	:	Arachnida
Order	:	Acarina
Family	:	Tetranychidae
Genus	:	*Polyphagotarsonemus*
Species	:	*latus* (Banks).

Status of the pest: It is an occasional pest causing damage to mulberry crop in the states of Tamil Nadu, Uttarakhand and Jammu & Kashmir.

Seasonal incidence: Generally yellow mite infestation is stray and sporadic. The infestation starts in the first week of August during monsoon season from border row plants and increases gradually to adjoining plants in middle rows.

Nature of Damage

- Attacks apical leaves and causes retardation of growth in plants.
- Leaves become corky, brittle, wrinkled, shrunken in size, lose its green and glossy appearance, lose chlorophyll content.

Management

- Clipping and collecting the mite infested apical tender mulberry shoot in polythene bag and burning them.
- Removing weeds from the mulberry plots to prevent the alternate hosts and migration of mites.
- Two spray of 0.2 per cent Dicofol @200 litre/acre at an interval of 15 days is effective to contain the mite population (safe period: 12 days after 2nd spray).

(28) COCKCHAFER BEETLE

Holotrichia serrata, H. rufoflava and *Schizonycha ruficollis* are the common grubs that affect mulberry plants. The larvae of these grubs are also known as white grub while adults are called chafers.

Taxonomic Position

Class	:	Insecta
Order	:	Coleoptera
Family	:	Scarabaeidae
Genus	:	*Holotrichia*
Species	:	*serrata* (Fab.)

Status of the pest: It is an occasional pest causing damage to mulberry crops in Karnataka, Kerala and Tamil Nadu.

Biology: The female lays eggs in soil up to depth of 10 cm. The newly hatched grubs initially feed on organic matter but as they grow, they feed on roots or rootlets causing damage to mulberry plants. The full-grown larvae are white, having brown head and prominent thoracic legs and measures 35 mm in length. The adult beetles are dull brown. The incubation period lasts for 7-10 days. Larval development is completed in 50-65 days. After monsoon, the full-grown larvae migrate to a considerable depth in soil for pupation. Larval development passing from first to third instar, takes one year. The pupa is creamy white and semicircular. Pupal period lasts for 15 days. They emerge after first rain. The beetles conceal themselves in the soil and come out for feeding at night.

Seasonal incidence: They occur mostly during May-June. This is the reason, they are also known as May-June beetles.

Nature of Damage

- Adults are nocturnal. They enter into mulberry garden as a swarm during night and devastate entire garden by feeding all the foliages and leaving stem portion alone.

Management

- Collection and killing of emerged adults after first monsoon rains.
- Installation of light trap and collection of adult beetles during night in kerosinized water container.
- Ploughing and hoeing after first summer rains to expose the different stages of the pest to natural enemies.
- Foliar application of 0.2 per cent (2.63 ml per litter of water) DDVP (safe period - 17 days) or 0.2 per cent (2 ml per litre of water) Neem oil (safe period - 12 days).

- Soil application of 0.2 per cent Malathion or Chloropyriphos dust in white grub areas.

(29) WASP CATERPILLAR

(i) Amata passalis: Commonly known as wasp moth is a minor pest of mulberry.

Taxonomic Position

Class	:	Insecta
Order	:	Lepidoptera
Family	:	Amatidae
Genus	:	*Amata*
Species	:	*passalis* (Fab.)

Status of the pest: It damages the mulberry crop throughput the country.

Biology: Female lays about 500 eggs. The laid eggs are round in shape and are attached to the ventral side of mulberry leaves. They are white in colour but gradually change to yellow and finally turn to dark brown before hatching. Incubation period is 6-7 days. Newly hatched caterpillars are dull white in colour. Thin brownish hairs are found all over the body of the caterpillars. The larvae are active and scrap the chlorophyll layer of the leaf. With the advancement of growth, the colour of the larvae also changes to brown and larvae starts feeding on the mulberry leaves. The full-grown caterpillar measures 20-25 mm in length. There are four moults and larval period is 32 days. The caterpillar pupates inside the folds of leaves within the silken web. The pupa measures 14-18 mm in length and the colour of the pupa is pink. Pupal duration is about 10-12 days. Adult males are elongate with narrow and slender abdomen whereas the females are stout and bulky. Wings of adults are brownish black in colour. Forewings have seven transparent spots. Life cycle completes in 48-51 days. Mating takes place after about 15 hrs of emergence and egg laying starts after 8-10 hrs of copulation (Singh, 1972).

Seasonal incidence: Pest occurs mostly during February - August.

Nature of Damage

- Branches of mulberry plants are noticed without leaves.
- Pest attack leads to reduction in leaf yield.

Management

- Collection and destruction of egg masses and young gregarious caterpillars.
- Application of 0.2 per cent DDVP (2 ml/litre of water) (Dimethyl Dichloro Vinyl Phosphate).
- Safe period for use of mulberry leaves for feeding to silkworm is 17 days after spray/application.

(ii) Ceryx godarti: A minor pest of mulberry commonly known as wasp moth.

Taxonomic Position

Class	:	Insecta
Order	:	Lepidoptera
Family	:	Amatidae
Genus	:	*Ceryx*
Species	:	*godarti* (Bdv.)

Status of the pest: The pest is found damaging the mulberry crops throughout the country.

Biology: Female moth lays about 130-235 eggs in batches, which are deposited on the lower surface of the tender leaves. Eggs are round in shape and pale yellow in colour. The incubation period of eggs is about 5 days after which larvae hatches. Freshly hatched larvae are light brown in colour and bear hairs on all the segments of the body. Larvae undergo four moults. Fully-grown larvae are 22-25 mm in length. Mature larvae are almost dark in colour covered with hairs. Larval period is approximately 30 days. Pupation takes place under dry leaves and a thin flabby cocoon is made out of its hairs. Size of the pupa is 11-14 mm and pupal period is 12-13 days after which adults emerges from the pupae. Adult males are with narrow abdomen whereas females are with broad abdomen. The female is stouter. The moths are very active and are found to be diurnal in habit. Pillai (1968 b) studied the bionomics of the pest in detail.

Seasonal incidence: The pest occurs during February - August. Mulberry plants without leaves are observed in the field affected with the pest. This leads to reduction in leaf yield.

Nature of Damage

- The young larvae skeletonise the leaves by scrapping the chlorophyll.
- Full-grown larvae feed on whole leaves.

Management

- Collection and destruction of egg masses and young gregarious caterpillars.
- Application of 0.2 per cent DDVP. Safe period for use of mulberry leaves for feeding to silkworm is 17 days after spray/application.

(30) LEAF WEBBER *(Glyphodes pyloalis)*

Taxonomic Position

Class	:	Insecta
Order	:	Lepidoptera
Genus	:	*Glyphodes*
Species	:	*pyloalis*

Status of the pest: It is a minor pest of mulberry. The intensity of damage is mostly high (13.86%) during September month.

Biology: The adults are light silvery cream in colour, beautifully ornamented with black decorative markings at the edge and middle of the wings. The young larvae are pale green with faint brown spots on either side of the dorsal part. The larval body is devoid of hair. On maturity, the larvae develop four dark black spots on each segment. Pupation takes place inside the folded leaf. The mature larva makes a fine net like cover before pupation. The pupa is elongate, dark brown in colour and 1.0-1.2 cm in length. The adult comes out from the pupa after 10 days of pupation.

Seasonal incidence: Causing damage to mulberry throughout the year.

Nature of Damage

- Leaf turns brown, wither and fall.
- Growth of the plant ceases.
- The mature worm folds lamina marginally in 4th and 5th leaves of the shoot resultantly; major portion of the leaf blade is lost.

Management

- Spray of DDVP (0.15%) twice a month at 15 days interval.

(31) RED WEAVER ANT *(Oecophylla smaragdina)*

Oecophylla smaragdina is commonly known as weaver ant as they construct nest by sewing leaves together using silken threads. The nest is a mixture of silk, live and dead leaves. The ants are mostly aerial and respond to vibration of the nest by furious activity and attack field workers. It makes nests on trees such as mango, coconut, cocoa, ficus, gliricidia etc. In mulberry, about 20-25 nests of different sizes can be formed depending on the size of the plant.

Taxonomic Position

Class	:	Insecta
Order	:	Hymenoptera
Family	:	Formicidae
Genus	:	*Oecophylla*
Species	:	*smaragdina* (Fab.)

Status of the pest: It is a minor pest of mulberry.

Biology: The life cycle of the weaver ant has four stages namely egg, larva, pupa and adult. The queen ant starts the ants' nest/colonies. Once mated, it looks for a nest site, gets rid of wings and seals herself into a small chamber and lays small batch of eggs. The queen is located in one nest and the eggs in different nest where workers and soldier ants are found. The workers are females and the soldiers are larger. Fertilized eggs develop into females and queen and unfertilised into males. As the colony reaches maturity it begins to produce queens and males for next generation. Males can remain in the nest for some months and most of them die after leaving the nest. Adults are reddish to brown and have 10-segmented antennae with two segmented clubs. The eyes are large. They do not have stingers but can give painful bite due to chemical secretion from their abdomen. The life cycle spans for 8-10 weeks.

Seasonal incidence: Causing damage to mulberry throughout the year.

Nature of Damage

- They attack growing tips, foliage and reproductive parts and young shoots.
- Folds the leaf and hence reduces the photosynthesis resulting in poor quality and quantity of leaf.
- Economic Threshold is about 15-20 per cent in terms of dry leaf, retarded growth of shoot and formation of nest around other branches of infected plants (Tikader and Thangavelu, 2003).

Management

- Ploughing and digging after crop harvest helps in reducing the ant nests.
- Repeated pruning, which is generally followed for foliage production in mulberry, directly or indirectly help to reduce the red ant incidence.
- Apply 5 per cent Heptachlor dust @ 10 kg/acre at two weeks interval (safe period – 15 days).
- Spray of dieldrin or Malathion (0.2%), at two weeks interval (safe period – 21 days).

(32) SPITTLE BUGS *(Clovia puncta)*

They are best known for their unusual habit of forming masses of spittle. The spittle-bug is popularly known as Cockoo-spits.

Taxonomic Position

Class	:	Insecta
Order	:	Homoptera
Family	:	Cercopidae
Genus	:	*Clovia*
Species	:	puncta (Walker).

Status of the pest: It is a minor pest of mulberry in Karnataka.

Biology: The adult bug lay 30-90 eggs on mulberry branches. Hatched nymphs attached themselves with host leaf with their stylets. The young ones start forming spittle masses for the excess plant juice they feed on. Nymphs undergo moults four times in their spittle. The nymph derives its nourishment from plant sap. The adults have full developed wings. Female ovipositor and male genitalia are well developed. There will be 2 to 3 generations in a year.

Seasonal incidence: Occurrence of this insect is on higher side during winter months compared to summer.

Nature of damage: Nymph sucks out the plant juice and excrete the excess out which is mixed with viscid fluid secreted from the glands on the 7th & 8th segments. The nymph on the food plants remain concealed under a mass of froth or the so called cuckoo-spits. The spittle-bug affected leaves appeared 'desaped' and has reduced leaf palatability.

Management

- Collect and destroy leaf with spittle-bug nymphs by burning.
- Apply 0.15 per cent Neem pesticide with 0.03 per cent Azadirachtin to kill nymphs.

(33) LEAF TIER/BELL MOTH *(Archips micaceana)*

Taxonomic Position

Class	:	Lepidoptera
Family	:	Tortricidae
Genus	:	*Archips*
Species	:	*micaceana.*

Status of the pest: It is a minor pest affecting crop throughout the country.

Biology: Female moth lays 80-100 eggs with many clutches. The greenish yellow egg hatches after 6 days of incubation. It undergoes five larval stages within the leaf fold. The pupal period lasts for 6-8 days.

Seasonal incidence: It occurs throughout the year. The peak of incidence is from January to March.

Nature of damage: Infest tender apical shoots. Larvae feed by scrapping the leaf epidermis.

Management

- Clipping and destroying the pest infested branches.

- Foliar application of 0.076 per cent DDVP (76% EC) 2 to 3 times with 10 days interval. Safe period 7 days of last spray.
- Release of egg parasitoid, *Trichogramma chilonis* @ one lakh adults/acre in four split doses (June-July; August-September; October-November and January-February).

(B) NON-INSECT PESTS

(1) NEMATODES *(Meloidogyne incognita)*

About 42 species belonging to 24 genera of nematodes are found associated with mulberry in different mulberry growing areas of the world (Govindaiah *et al.*, 1989). The severity of attack and extent of damage depends on the soil and climatic conditions of the area. The important species infesting mulberry are *Meloidogyne incognita, M. incognita, M. javanica, M. arenaria, M. hapla, Criconemella sp., Helicotylenchus sp., Hemicriconemoides sp., Hoplolaimus sp. etc. Meloidogyne incognita* is the most common polyphagous pest, distributed worldwide and found abundantly in tropical and sub-tropical countries.

Taxonomic Position

Phylum	:	Nematoda
Class	:	Secerentia
Order	:	Tylenchia
Family	:	Heteroderoidae
Genus	:	*Meloidogyne*
Species	:	*incognita* (Kofoid & White).

Status of the pest: This pest is affecting mulberry crop in all the seasons throughout the country.

Biology: There are three stages in the life cycle of nematode *i.e.* egg, larva and adult. Female lays 300-500 eggs covered with gelatinous substance. The eggs are ellipsoidal with a diameter of 40-45 µm and length of 90-100 µm. In favourable season, eggs hatch and larvae are liberated in the soil. The second stage juvenile larvae are vermiform with 15-20 µm diameter and 400-450 µm length. The second stage female larvae enter into the roots through root tips by making hole with the help of their stylet and harbour in subepidermal layer. Soon after the entry, it starts feeding on the parenchymatous cells. Due to the process of hypertrophy and hyperplasia induced by the nematode, characteristic knots appear on the roots. Larva undergoes four moults and develops into mature egg laying female. Reproduction takes place mostly by parthenogenesis and very rarely by sexual means, as occurrence of male is very rare. It takes 30-40 days to complete the life cycle. The nematode passes through six generations a year. Temperature from 15-35°C (optimum being 20-30°C), soil humidity of more than 60 per cent and soil pH of 4-8 are favourable for the development of nematode. It is more common in sandy type of soils under irrigated conditions.

Seasonal incidence: It can occur at any time of the year in sandy type of soils low in organic matter under irrigated conditions. The severity of the disease increases with increased age of the garden.

Nature of Damage

- The affected plants show stunted growth, marginal necrosis and leaf chlorosis, yellowing, wilting, patching etc.
- Underground symptoms include formation of characteristic galls or knots on the roots.
- The nematode damaged roots do not utilize water and fertilizers as effectively as healthy parts resulting in poor plant growth, in turn leading to about 15 per cent leaf yield loss in addition to loosing the quality of the leaves (Govindaiah *et al.*, 1991).

Economic Threshold Level (ETL) and crop losses: *M. incognita* is found to be highly pathogenic to mulberry causing significant reduction in plant growth and leaf yield. At 1000 larvae/plant or 150 larvae/250 cc soil under field conditions is the ETL. The avoidable leaf yield loss is estimated up to 15 per cent (Govindaiah *et al.*, 1991). Besides reducing the leaf production, it also affects the nutritive value by reducing the protein content, which is an important nutrient for silkworm growth.

Management

Any strategy to control of nematodes depends on the crop cycle, total life span and cropping pattern. Mulberry being a perennial crop, the crop rotation becomes unpractical. Hence, control at the initial stages by different integrated approaches becomes very important.

- Deep digging or ploughing of infested mulberry garden during summer exposes the nematode eggs and larvae to direct sun, which kills the nematodes.
- Application of neem oil cake @ 2 tonne/ha/yr in four equal split doses followed by application of Carbofuron 3 G @ 3 kg/ha/year to the soil.
- Intercropping of nematicidal plants like marigold (*Tagetus patula*) and sun hemp (*Crotalaria spectabilis*) @ 10 per square meter between mulberry rows and later on mulching of the same in soil provides additional organic matter to the soil besides controlling the pest. When the nematode enters into the root system of these plants, they get imprisoned because of the formation of thick coat of antinematic substances (Belcher and Hussey, 1977).
- Application of nematicide *viz.*, Temic 10 G (Aldicarb) or Furadon 3 G (Carbofuran) @ 30 kg/ha/yr in four equal split doses along with fertilizers at an interval of 3 months and mixing it well in the soil while digging

followed by regular irrigation controls the pest. After 40-45 days of nematicide application, the leaves can be used for silkworm rearing.

- Mulching of green leaves of neem (*Azadirachta indica*) and Pongamia (*Pongamia pinnnata*) at 1 tonne/acre/crop is also effective in the control of root-knot nematode population (Govindaiah *et al.*, 1989).
- Talc based bionematicide (Bionema) along with neem oil cake reduces pest infestation considerably.
- S13, S30, S1096, RFS135 and V1 moderately resistant mulberry varieties can commercially be exploited.
- Destroy all the weeds around the mulberry garden so that freshly hatched second stage larvae die due to starvation because weeds are considered as the carrier of nematodes and also help them in multiplication.

(2) SNAIL: Snails are considered minor pest. They are acting as defoliator not only on agricultural and horticultural crops but also to mulberry. Among the mulberry infesting snails *Helix aspersa, Acatina fulica* (Pila) and *Cochliopa* species are most common.

Taxonomic Position

Phylum	:	Mollusca
Class	:	Gastropoda
Sub-class	:	Heterobranchia
Family	:	Stylomatophora
Genus	:	*Helix*
Species	:	*aspersa* (Müller).

Status of the pest: It is a minor pest of mulberry.

Biology: A hard shell, usually marked with spirals, protects the snail body. Most land snails are nocturnal, but following a rain may come out of their hiding places during the day. They move with a gliding motion by means of a long flat muscular organ called a foot. Mucus, constantly secreted by glands in the foot, facilitates movement and leaves silver like slimy trail. The reproductive organs of both sexes occur in the same individuals and each is capable of self-fertilization, although cross-fertilization is normal. The mollusc develops completely in a year's time but its mating capacity commences from the third year. Mating continues for 4-12 hours. Snails start laying eggs 2 to 3 weeks after mating. Snails lay up to 100 eggs in their first year and up to 500 in their second year. Fecundity declines after the second year but snails may live up to five years with a total egg clutch of up to 1000. The egg mass is concealed by a mixture of soil with secreted mucus followed by a quantity of excrement. Frequency of oviposition is subject to temperature, humidity, and soil conditions. Low temperature and low humidity inhibit the activity of the snail. During warm damp weather, oviposition may be as frequent as once a month. Low humidity and cold temperatures greatly inhibit the activity of the snails. The egg measure 1.5-2.5 cm in diameter and are yellowish in colour. The egg hatches out at 20-25°C temperature into young ones along with the shell within 10-12 days. The young ones grow into adult, which is found active during rainy and winter season and aestivates during other seasons. It shrinks its body and keeps inside the shell for 5-7 months during hibernation. It lives for 5-6 years.

Seasonal incidence: Severe incidence of the pest starts with onset of monsoon.

Nature of Damage

- During the sunny hours of the day, snails either rest on the pruned mulberry clumps or on wood plants and during the late evening hours and whole night they crawl on the foliage in large number and feed on the leaves both from the margin and centre.

Giant African snail infestation

Management

- Periodic cleaning of the sewage/drain canal and or river banks adjacent to mulberry farms.
- Plough the land deeply so that the eggs laid in the inner surface of the soil gets exposed to direct sunlight and killed.
- Encouraging the natural predators of the molluscs like lizards, frogs and birds.
- During summer when the snails are not active collect them near sand beds, farmyard manure heaps and under leaf surfaces and destroy them by crushing or burying.
- During rainy (late monsoon) when they keep coming out from their hiding place, 25 per cent salt solution (mix 1 kg of salt in 4 litres of water) is sprayed on them. Due to this spray, the snails imbibe the salt solution, vomits and finally collapse. Water should be sprayed on mulberry plants within half an hour of

salt solution spraying to protect the plant from damage.

- Lime powder can be dusted on boarders of the garden and between rows after sunset so that the snails get killed sticking on to the lime powder.
- As a chemical control before planning, the mulberry cuttings are dipped into metaldehyde solution for few minutes or metaldehyde mixed along with wheat brawn can be sprinkled on soil to prevent infestation.

Natural Enemies: In nature, natural enemies of insect pests such as pathogens, parasitoids and predators are working continuously against crop pests. However, time has come that these natural enemies are mass produced in the laboratories and introduced to field to strengthen the hands of already existing natural enemies to get more pronounced result in control of these noxious pets. Some of the natural enemies of mulberry pests are presented (Table 2.10) here.

Table 2.10: Natural Enemies of Mulberry Pests

S.N.	Pests	Parasitoids	Predators
1.	Mealy bug (*Maconellicoccus hirsutus*)	*Anagyrus kamali* (Nymphal parasitoid)	*Cryptolaemus montrouzieri*, *Scymnus coccivora*
2.	Bihar hairy caterpillar (*Spilarctia obliqua*)	*Meteoras dichomeridis* (Larval parasitoid), *Trichogramma chilonis* (Egg parasitoid)	*Eocanthecona furcellata*
3.	Leaf roller (*Diaphania pulverulentalis*)	*Trichogramma chilonis* (Egg parasitoid), *Tetrastichus howardii* (Pupal parasitoid), *Apanteles* sp. (Larval parasitoid)	*Calosoma sp.*, *Eocanthecona furcellata*

Table 2.11 : Botanical Bio-pesticides Presently in Use

Product	Manufacturer	Applied on	Pests Target	Price (Rs.)
Achook	Godrey Agrovet Ltd, Mumbai	Gram, cotton, paddy and vegetables like cauliflowers	Whiteflies, mites, jassids, thrips, borers, aphids, caterpillars	220/litre
Bio-2001	Bicco Agro Products, Private Ltd, Kolkata	Cotton, tea, mustard, coffee, sugarcane	Mites, aphids, thrips, jassids	240/litre
Bio-neem	Bicco Agro Products, Private Ltd, Kolkata	Cotton, paddy, mustard, vegetables	Whiteflies, borers, aphids, caterpillar diamond moth	260/litre
Neem gold	Southern Petro-chemical Industries Corporation Ltd, Chennai	Cotton, paddy, pulses, vegetables like potato	Whiteflies, borers, aphids, caterpillars, thrips, diamond back moth	200/litre
TR MIT	Bicco Agro Products, Private Ltd, Kolkata	Cotton, paddy, mustard, sugarcane	Termites	200/kg.
Gronim	National Tree Growers Coopera-tive Federation Ltd., Gujarat	Cotton, chilli, grapes, apple, peas, papaya, potato	Sugarcane borer, cotton bollworms	260/kg.
Neemarin	Biotech International Ltd., New Delhi	Cotton, pulses, cereals	Whiteflies, borers, aphids, caterpillars, thrips	290/litre

Use of Bio-pesticides in Control of Pest

Around 739 MT of neem-based bio-pesticide and at least 135 MT of Bt based bio-pesticides are used every year under IPM programme in order to combat with various pest problems. However, some of the products *i.e.* Biolep, Biovirus-S, Vertical and Bio-Dart in the form of microbial bio-pesticides are available in the market and are being used in controlling insect pests in agriculture, horticulture and ornamental plants. But, these products cannot be used against the insect pests in the mulberry eco-system, as the silkworm larvae are susceptible to them. However, some of the common botanical pesticides available in the market and their sources are given in Table 2.11, which can be tried in the control of insect pest of mulberry also.

READY RECKONER FOR CHEMICAL & BIOLOGICAL CONTROL

Ready reckoner is always helpful in control of pest population at correct time in the field. The ready reckoner for biological and chemical control measures of some of the most important mulberry pests are presented in Table 2.12 and 2.13 respectively.

Table 2.12: Ready Reckoner for Biological Control of Some Mulberry Pests

S.N.	Name of the pest	Name of the bio-control agent	Release rate/acre
1.	Mealy bug	*Cryptolaemus montrouzieri*,	250
		Scymnus coccivora	500
2.	Leaf roller	*Trichogramma chilonis*,	1 Lakh
		Tetrastichus howardii	1 Lakh
3.	Bihar hairy caterpillar	*Trichogramma chilonis*	1 Lakh

Table 2.13: Ready Reckoner for Chemical Control of Mulberry Pests

S.No.	Name of the pest	Insecticide (EC %)	Required concentration (%)	Quantity / litre of water	Safe period (days)
1.	Mealy bug	DDVP 76%	0.20	2.63 ml	17
2.	Leaf roller	DDVP 76%	0.076	1.0 ml	7
3.	Bihar hairy caterpillar	DDVP 76%	0.15	2.0 ml	9
4.	Jassids	DDVP 76%	0.076	1.0 ml	8
		Dimethoate 30%	0.10	3.3 ml	6
5.	Thrips	Dimethoate 30%	0.20	6.6 ml	10
6.	Scale insects	Diesel and soap emulsion	1:3	-	-
		DDVP 76%	0.15	2.0 ml	9
7.	Grasshoppers	DDVP 76%	0.15	2.0 ml	9
8.	Stem girdler	DDVP 76%	0.20	2.63 ml per injection	17
9.	Termites	Chloropyriphos 20%	0.08	2.0 ml	12

3

CHAPTER

Mulberry Diseases

Mulberry (*Morus* spp.), the sole food plant for rearing of silkworm (*Bombyx mori* L.) is grown under wide range of ecological conditions. During the growth, like any other plant, various types of pathogens causing diseases such as fungi, bacteria, mycoplasma, viruses and nematodes also affect mulberry. Diseases, which are the main constraints in leaf production, are caused either by pathogens (Sastry, 1984) or non-pathogens. Among pathogens leaf spot (fungal and bacterial), powdery mildew, leaf rust and root knot are most common diseases, which causes economically significant loss.

Foliar diseases of mulberry affect leaf yield as well as leaf quality resulting in poor cocoon crop and consequent reduction in the income of the rearers. Leaf yield loss due to leaf spot, powdery mildew and leaf rust disease has been reported to be the tune of 46.8 per cent, 20.45 per cent and 17.35 per cent respectively during the respective seasons. Besides, these diseases also affects leaf quality leading to poor silkworm rearing and crop loss up to 54.58 per cent and 55.59 per cent at maximum severity of leaf spot and powdery mildew fetching income reduction of Rs. 13,041 and Rs.17, 291/ha respectively. Diseased mulberry leaves are poor in proteins, sugars and moisture. As most of the farmers in India are marginal and small farmers having limited land holding, the loss due to the diseases cannot be underestimated and appropriate plant protection measures are necessary to boost effectively mulberry foliage production.

Classification of mulberry diseases: The disease may be infectious or non-infectious. All the diseases caused by pathogenic/parasitic organisms such as fungi, bacteria, mycoplasma, virus etc multiply in their host and spread to others are called infectious while those caused by deficiency of nutrients, extreme temperature, moisture etc are non-infectious diseases.

(A) Infectious Diseases or Pathogenic Diseases: Pathogenic organisms under a set of suitable environmental of conditions incite these diseases. The pathogenic organisms mostly responsible for plant diseases are—fungi, bacteria, mycoplasma, virus and nematode (Table 3.1).

(B) Non-infectious or Non-pathogenic or Physiological Diseases: These diseases are caused by mineral excess or mineral deficiency in the soil, unfavourable temperature, moisture, air pollution etc (Table 3.2). The diseases remain non-infectious and are not transmitted from one plant to another healthy plant.

Table 3.1 : Infectious Diseases or Pathogenic Diseases

Name of diseases	Pathogen	Season
1. Fungal diseases		
(i) Major diseases		
Powdery mildew	*Phyllactinia corylea* *Ovulariopsis sp.*	Winter/spring
Leaf rust	*Peridiopsora mori* *Caeoma mori* *Aecidium mori* *Cerotelium fici*	Winter/spring
Leaf spot	*Myrothecium rorridum* *Myrothecium mori* *Pseudocercospora mori* *P. moracearwn* *P. garhwalensis* *Cercospora moricola*	Rainy/Autumn

(ii) Minor diseases		
Phloeospora leaf spot	*Phleospora maculens*	Rainy/Autumn
Fusarium leaf spot	*Fusarium concolor*	Rainy
Twig blight	*Fusarium pallidoroseum*	Rainy
Bud blight	*Fusarium solani*	Winter
Leaf blight	*Alterneria alternata,*	Autumn/Winter
	Alterneria tenuissima	
Sooty mould/stem blight	*Meliola amphitricha*	Rainy
Stem canker	*Botryodiploidia theobromae*	Rainy Rainy
Armilaria root rot	*Armilaria mellea*	Rainy
Violet root rot	*Helicobasidium mompa*	Rainy
White root rot	*Rosellinia necatrix*	Rainy
Collar rot	*Phoma mororum*	
Black root rot	*Lasiodiplodia theobromae*	
Dry root rot	*Fusarium solani*	
	Fusarium oxysporum	
Charcoal rot	*Macrophomina*	
	phaseolina	Rainy
(2) Bacterial diseases		
Mulberry blight	*Pseudomonas mori*	Rainy
Bacterial leaf spot/blight	*Xanthomonas mori*	Rainy
Bacterial wilt/bacterial root rot	*Pseudomonas solanacearum*	Rainy
(3) Virus diseases		
Mosaic disease	Virus	Rainy
Yellow net vein disease	Virus	Rainy
(4) Mycoplasma disease		
Dwarf disease	Mycoplasma	Rainy
(5) Nematode disease		
Root knot	*Meloidogyne incognita*	Rainy/Autumn

Table 3.2 : Non-infectious Diseases or Non-pathogenic or Physiological Diseases

Mineral deficiency		Temperature effect	Soil moisture disturbance	Air pollution
Macronutrient	**Micronutrient**	High Temperature	Flooding	Sulphur dioxide, Oxides of Nitrogen and Fluorides
Nitrogen	Iron	Low Temperature	Drought	
Phosphorus	Boron			
Potassium	Manganese			
Calcium	Zinc			
Sulphur	Copper			
Magnesium	Molybdenum			

[A] INFECTIOUS DISEASES OR PATHOGENIC DISEASES

(1) FUNGAL DISEASES

(*a*) MAJOR DISEASES

(*i*) POWDERY MILDEW (*Phyllactinia corylea*)

Phyllactinia corylea (Pers.) is the most common, serious and wide spread pathogen of mulberry causing powdery mildew disease in India and known to occur in almost all the mulberry growing areas of the world. It causes extensive damage to the foliage and reduces feeding quality of leaf, more precisely to mention that it decreases protein and moisture contents of leaves due to luxuriant mycelial growth on the lower surface, which also affects silkworm growth and development adversely.

Taxonomic Position

Order	:	Erysiphales
Class	:	Ascomycetes
Family	:	Erysiphaceae
Genus	:	*Phyllactinia*
Species	:	*corylea* (Pers.)

Symptoms

- The quality of the infected leaves deteriorates.
- Appearance of white powdery patches on the ventral surface of the leaves. Corresponding to these patches on the dorsal surface, the leaves turn chlorotic.
- Infected leaves become yellowish, loose moisture becomes coarse and less nutritive and turns leathery due to loss of water.
- Infection on young leaves causes curling, crinkling, reduction in leaf width and longitudinal folding.
- As the disease advances the patches spread to the entire leaf surface and turns to blackish colour due to growth of hyperparasite on the mildew fungus.
- The disease slows down the oxidation process and reduces the production of carbohydrates and nitrogenous matter.
- Premature defoliation occurs. The loss incited by the pathogen ranges from 3.03-12.53 per cent in Karnataka (Gunasekhar *et al.*, 1994) and 3.22-24.0 per cent in West Bengal (Quadri *et al.*, 1998).
- Histopathological and histochemical studies reveal that mesophyll tissues of the infected leaf become hypertrophied, causing increase in leaf thickness and that in advanced stage gradually decreases in size leading to hyperplasia.

Seasonal incidence: In temperate region and subtropical hills, where the temperature is mild, the disease prevails throughout the active growth period of mulberry *i.e.* from spring (March-April) to autumn (September-October). However, in tropical and sub-tropical plains, where the temperature is comparatively hot, the disease appears noticeably in July or August. Maximum severity is observed during October-December. Close spacing of plants and excessive application of nitrogenous fertilizer favours disease severity.

Pathogen and disease cycle: The disease is commonly known as powdery mildew or white back disease (Itoi *et al.*, 1960). The pathogen is an ectoparasite. The disease is caused by *Phyllactinia corylea* (Pers.). It is more prevalent in hilly areas than in plains. Disease occurs mostly during rainy and winter season (July-March). Feeding of mildew-affected leaves to silkworm adversely affects the growth and development of silkworm resulting in poor cocoon yield and silk quality (Nomani *et al.*, 1970; Sullia and Padma, 1987). Temperature ranging between 20-27°C is optimal for infection and disease development, whereas, temperature above 35°C inhibits the conidial germination. Subsequently, its occurrence was reported from all major mulberry-growing areas (Ramkrishanan and Sundaram, 1954; Bakshi and Singh, 1961, Rangaswami *et al.*, 1970). The mycelium is hyaline, septate and unbranched, which is usually superficial on the ventral surface of leaf. It spreads all over the ventral surface of the leaves and absorbs the nutrients by sending special type of intracellular hyphae (haustoria) through the stomata of the leaves. The haustoria are finger shaped and irregular. The fungus reproduces by both asexual and sexual methods. Asexual reproduction takes place through conidia during the favourable conditions. Conidia are borne terminally on the septate conidiophores. Conidiophores are straight, erect and hyaline with inflated tips. Dispersal of conidia is more during cloudy rainy days than bright sunny days (Krishna Prasad and Siddaramaiah, 1979; Biswas *et al.*, 1993). Conidia are hyaline, unicellular; club shaped measuring 20×70 μ each borne on conidiophores. Sexual reproduction takes place by means of fusion of antheridium and ascogonium, which form the cleistothecia inside which 5-50 asci are seen. Ascus is short, pedicellate, cylindrical, hyaline, 60-105 × 20-40μ in size and mostly contains 2-3 ascospores. In favourable conditions, ascus breaks open and releases ascospores. The ascospores on reaching the host germinate and start primary infection. Secondary infection takes place through production of conidia.

Powdery mildew

Predisposing factors: 24-28°C atmospheric temperature and 60-70 per cent relative humidity.

Control Measures

Varietal resistance: The severity of disease depends on the degree of susceptibility of mulberry plants. So raising of mulberry genotypes with resistant variety should be considered first in adopting any management system. Therefore, mulberry varieties like S-54, S-36, MR-2, Kosen, Philippine, Italian and Papua resistant to powdery mildew are to be cultivated or used in breeding programmes.

Cultural control: Wider spacing, good irrigation and weeding will reduce the intensity of mildew to a great extent. Growing of unwanted trees in and around the mulberry garden is to be avoided as shade condition in mulberry garden promotes the disease development. Pruning of mulberry has beneficial effect in many respects including this disease control. In case of severe infection, pruning of branches is required before adopting any chemical control measure.

Biological control: Coccinellid insect, *Illeus indica* (Lady Bird Beetle) as well as fungal hyperparasite *Cladosporium* sp. have been reported as biological agents for control of powdery mildew (Bheemanna *et al.*, 1990).

Chemical control: Spray of any of the following fungicides is effective for control of mildew:

(*a*) Carbendazim (Bavistin 50 WP) 0.1 or 0.15 per cent twice at fifteen intervals (safe period: 15 days from the date of spray). One gram of Carbendazim is to be dissolved in one litre of water. 60-80 litres of solution is required to spray one acre of mulberry garden. Spraying should be carried during the cool hours of the day that is preferably in the morning. It should not be sprayed in the afternoon and during rainy days.

(*b*) Wettable sulphur (Sulfex 80 WP) 0.2 per cent Conc. (safe period—14 days).

(*c*) Dinocarp (Karathane) 0.2 per cent or Morestan 0.1 per cent (safe period—20 days)

While spraying the fungicides, the lower surface of the leaves should be thoroughly drenched.

- Apply sufficient quantity of basic fertilizer and maintain timely top dressing with a mixture of potash fertilizer. Also, to preclude desiccation during long dry period or drought, irrigate to increase plant vigour.
- Several plant extracts, although found effective in minimizing the intensity of disease in mulberry, there use in field as fungicides requires more studies.

(ii) Mulberry Rust: Two types of rust *i.e.* leaf rust and red rust found affecting mulberry plantation.

(*a*) **Brown leaf rust** (*Peridiospora mori*): It is a common disease in regions having temperate climate while in plains it appears during winter and post winter season (November-February). Rust disease is influenced by environmental factors, host range and genotype. Temperature range of 22-26°C and high relative humidity above 70 per cent are favourable for the rust development in plants.

Taxonomic Position

Order	:	Uredinales
Class	:	Imperfecti
Family	:	Uredinaceae
Genus	:	*Peridiospora*
Species	:	*mori* (Barclay).

Symptoms

- Appearance of brownish pustules on lower (ventral) surface of the leaves with brown spots on the upper (dorsal) surface.
- Yellowing of the leaves.
- Leaves wither off.
- Reduction in moisture, crude protein, reducing sugars and total sugars.
- Premature leaves fall resulting in shortage of leaves during the late age rearing of silkworm (Biswas *et al.*, 2001).

Seasonal incidence: The disease is most common during winter months (November-January). Medium and coarse leaves are susceptible to infection. The loss due to this disease is estimated to be about 5-10 per cent.

Pathogen and disease cycle: The disease commonly known as leaf rust is caused by a fungal pathogen *Peridiospora mori* (Barclay). The disease is prevalent in all mulberry-growing countries of the world. The disease was first reported in India by Sydow and Buttler (1907) from Maharashtra and subsequently from other parts of the country by various workers. The rust is found to manifest itself on the lower surface of the leaves in the form of minute, reddish brown blister like pustules grouped together. The blister like pustules measure 0.4 - 0.5 mm in diameter. Each pustule is provided with a central ostiole through which spores ooze out. The pustules are uridinial sorus bearing sessile or sub-sessile urediniospores. Urediniospores disperse through water droplets and wind current. Long distance dissemina-tion of pathogen takes place through airborne uredinio-spores. Urediniospores remain viable months together under favourable conditions. Uredinia are ostiolate and are provided with peripheral thin periderm. The uridiniospores are sub-globose, oval to pyriform in shape. The germ tube prior to entering in the leaves produce characteristics aspersorium from which infection hyphae emerge. Infected leaves are unsuitable for silkworm feeding, affecting larval

Leaf rust disease

growth and all commercial characters of silkworm (Kumar *et al.*, 1993). Mature leaves are more susceptible to the disease than the tender ones. Rust severity is negatively correlated with both temperature and rainfall and spore release is higher during sunny days than cloudy days (Kumar *et al.*, 2000).

Predisposing Factors

- 15-30°C atmospheric temperature and 70-75 per cent relative humidity.

Control Measures

Varietal resistance: Resistance to leaf rust is very weak in mulberry. So far, none of the mulberry genotypes has been identified as completely resistant. However, mulberry varieties such as English black, Gosheoerami, Calabresa, Mizusuwa, Ichinose, RFS-135, S-13, S-25, S-30, S-35 and S-54 are reported to be moderately resistant.

Cultural control: Timely utilization of leaves especially during winter months and providing wider spacing and proper weeding will reduce the intensity of the disease. Inter cropping of soybean, green gram and foliage crops such as ragi, finger millet and maize between mulberry rows also reduces rust incidence (Prasad *et al.*, 1999).

Chemical control: Foliar spray of Carbendazim (Bavistin 50 WP) 0.2 per cent (safe period—7 days) and Foltaf 0.2 per cent. (Safe period—14 days) can reduce the disease severity. Spray may be repeated after 10 days, if required.

(*b*) Red/yellow rust (*Aecidium mori*): Red rust is widely distributed in the countries like China, Japan, Korea and USA of the temperate region. However, in India it is mainly confined to the sub-tropical hills of Darjeeling (West Bengal), Shillong (Meghalaya) and Shimla (Himachal Pradesh).

Taxonomic Position

Order	:	Uedinles
Class	:	Imperfectii
Family	:	Uredinaceae
Genus	:	*Aecidium*
Species	:	*mori* (Barcl.)

Symptoms

- Appear on the sprouting buds as yellow blister like patches.
- The affected veins or midribs become abnormal and curl up.
- Branch affected by disease becomes fragile and easily broken off.
- Infected buds becomes deformed and wrinkled without further growth and dropped off.
- A transverse section of the leaf through spots shows several aecia formed in clusters on both the surfaces and that on petiole and stem shows cluster of aecia on them (Biswas *et al.*, 2001).
- The disease reduces drastically the quality and quantity of leaf.

Seasonal incidence: The disease generally occurs at high altitude area with high rainfall. The disease is most common during spring (March-April) to autumn (September-October), although its prevalence is more during autumn in India. Maximum disease severity has been reported during September and October. It adversely affects the leaf yield and quality.

Pathogen and disease cycle: The disease commonly known as red rust is caused by fungal pathogen (*Aecidium mori*). About 80 per cent infection occurs from mycelia remaining in branch. Mycelium is septate, 4-6 μ in diameter with range colour particles and two nuclei in each cell, intracellular at initial stage producing haustoria. Haustoria are round or cylindrical having 7-15 μ diameters. Aecia are sub-epidermal, occurring mostly on upper surface of leaf, ball or pear like in shape, light yellow when young, become dark yellow or orange wit age having bell shaped openings mostly on the upper surface of the leaf. The aeciospores are disseminated by rain or wind on the host plant. After he aeciospore germinated, the tips of the germ tubes adhere tightly to the host epidermis and subsequently penetrate into the cuticle and the epidermal cells and later develop into mycelia. These mycelia spread into the host tissues and produce haustoria, which absorbs nutrients from the host cells. The fungus has only aeciospores in its life cycle and completes that within 20-30 days after reinfecting (Biswas *et al.*, 2001).

Predisposing Factors

- High altitude
- Regular and high rainfall
- 18-22°C atmospheric temperature and above 80 per cent humidity
- Susceptible mulberry varieties.

Control Measures

- Plantation of disease resistant mulberry varieties *viz.*, Kosan, Tr-10 and S-146.
- Pruning of mulberry plants during winter to eradicate over wintering mycelia remaining in the stem parts and to minimize the consequent disease incidence in the following year.
- Avoid dense planting to secure good aeration in the field.
- Fungicides like Bayleton (0.025%), Oxycarboxin/ Plantavax (0.05%), Zineb (0.2%) or Sapral (0.05%) are effective to control the disease if sprayed twice or thrice at 10-15 days interval.

- Bleaching powder solution (1%) can also be sprayed to eradicate the mature aecia when the disease appeared as prevalent.

(iii) Leaf Spot: Mulberry is affected by several leaf spot causing fungal pathogens. Literature survey has revealed about 18 fungal pathogens responsible for this disease (Table 3.3).

Table 3.3 : Pathogenic Fungi Causing Leaf Spot Disease in Mulberry in India

S. No.	Causing organism	Reported from	Reference
1.	*Alternaria alternata*	Mysore (Karnataka)	Gunasekhar & Govindaiah (1990)
2.	*Alternaria tenuissima*	Jammu (J & K)	Parotra (1960)
3.	*Atractum indicum*	Kalimpong (W.B.)	Kapoor & Munjal (1966)
4.	*Cercospora moricola*	Dharwar (Karnataka)	Patel *et al.* (1949)
5.	*Cercospora mori*	Delhi	Munjal *et al.* (1949)
6.	*Closterosporium mori*	Allahabad (U.P.)	Saksena (1928)
7.	*Coniothyrium albae*	Jammu (J & K)	Pandotra & Hussain (1960)
8.	*Drechslera yamaddai*	Meerut (U.P.)	Sharma (1974)
9.	*Fusarium concolor*	Chittor (Karnataka)	Reddy & Rao (1974)
10.	*Fusarium solani*	Jammu (J & K)	Chowdhary & Raj (1986)
11.	*Mycoshhaerella indica*	Poona (Maharashtra)	Viswanathan (1959)
12.	*Myrothecium roridum*	Mysore (Karnataka)	Govindaiah *et al.* (1989)

S. No.	Causing organism	Reported from	Reference
13.	*Phleospora maculans*	Bihar	Yadav (1963)
14.	*Phleospora mori*	J & K	Sydow & Butler (1916)
15.	*Phyllosticia morifolia*	J & K	Decosta & Munidkar (1948)
16.	*Pseudocercospora* v	Jaunpur (U.P.)	Srivastava & Srivastava (1975)
17.	*Sitasporium mori*	Meerut (U.P.)	Dublish & Singh (1976)
18.	*Stigmina obtecta*	Meerut (U.P.)	Dhar *et al.* (1988)

Grey (*Pseudocercospora)* **leaf spot**: *Pseudocercospora* leaf spot occurs widely all over the world. However, in most cases it is not considered as an important disease of mulberry, except in West Bengal, Bihar, Uttar Pradesh and Karnataka.

Taxonomic Position

Order : Moniliales

Class : Deuteromycetes

Family : Dematiaceae

Genus : *Pseudocercospora*

Species : *mori* (Hara)

Symptoms

- Appearance of grey to brown coloured spots on the ventral surface of the leaves which spreads upward.
- Spots coalesce in the later stages covering all over the ventral surface.
- Darkening of affected leaves.

- Premature leaf falls.
- Under microscope, the mildew like colonies of *Pseudocercospora* leaf spot consists of mycelia, conidiophores and conidia.

Seasonal incidence: The disease occurs throughout the year with high severity during winter months (November-January) and reduces the leaf production up to 5-10 per cent besides affecting the leaf quality.

Pathogen and disease cycle: The disease is caused by a fungal pathogen *Pseudocercospora mori* (Hara). The pathogen mycelium is in the form of branched, septate interwoven with large number of conidiophores. Mycelia may be external or internal. The conidiophores are brown in colour, branched and septate having chromonema. Conidiophores may vary in size from 100-200 mm in length. They develop in-group from external or internal mycelia. Each conidium measures 50-70 mm in length and 2-5 mm in breadth. Temperature ranging between 19-30°C favours the development of disease (Govindaiah *et al.*, 1990; Biswas *et al.*, 1996). The pathogen over-winters in the form of mycelia in plant debris or in soil. At the onset of warm weather, it rejuvenates and produces conidia. The conidia are borne by air to the ventral surface of lower leaves in mulberry for infection. Thereafter, secondary infection occurs by the conidia produced on the infected leaf surface, repeatedly.

Predisposing Factors

- The disease is air borne and spreads through conidia.
- 19-30°C atmospheric temperature and 70-75 per cent relative humidity favours the disease development.

Control Measures

Varietal resistance: No mulberry variety is completely resistant to grey spot disease. However, varieties like C-763, C-1726, S-1635, TR-10 and TR-4 are moderately resistant.

Cultural control: Avoid sprinkler irrigation. Wider spacing, proper irrigation and weeding will reduce the intensity of the disease.

Chemical control: Spray of any of the following fungicides is effective for control of leaf spot disease–

- Carbendazim (Bavistin 50% WP), 0.1 per cent concentration during early stage of infection (safe period–7 days).
- Mancozeb (Indofil M45), Indofil, 0.2 per cent (safe period: 14 days).

Cercospora leaf spot: A number of species of *Cercospora* are reported to cause leaf spot disease in mulberry. However, the name '*Cercospora* leaf spot' is mainly used for the disease, which is caused by *Cercospora moricola*. This disease is a major problem in mulberry when grown under tropical and subtropical conditions in plains. It is more prevalent in Karnataka, Andhra Pradesh, Tamil Nadu and Kerala, while in Uttarakhand, Uttar Pradesh, West Bengal, Jharkhand and Orissa, its occurrence is sporadic. Its occurrence is sporadic. The disease starts progressing on 30-40 days after pruning (DAP)/leaf harvesting and becomes severe on the 70th DAP.

Taxonomic Position

Order	:	Moniliales
Class	:	Deuteromycetes
Family	:	Dematiaceae
Genus	:	*Cercospora*
Species	:	*moricola* (Cooke).

Symptoms

- Appearance of small brownish irregular necrotic spots.
- Generally the disease affects tender leaves and its incidence increases with the increase in leaf age (Sukumar and Ramlingum, 1989).

- Reduced leaf moisture, protein, chlorophyll content and total sugars.
- Falling off of necrotic area from shoot holes on the leaves.
- Spots coalesce in the later stages.
- Increase in vanadium, silver, copper, molybdenum and gallium contents in infected leaves (Shree and Kumar, 1991).
- Premature leaf falls.

Predisposing Factors

- The disease is air borne and spreads by conidia primarily through rain droplets/splash.
- Temperature of 24-26°C and 70-80 per cent relative humidity are more congenial for the disease development.
- Prolonged moderate temperature, dew and 3-4 days of high humidity favour the severe infection.

***Cercospora* leaf spot**

Seasonal incidence: The disease is very common in rainy season (June-December) and prevails up to January - February (Siddaramaiah *et al.*, 1978). The optimal temperature of 24-26°C and prevalence of 70-80 per cent Relative Humidity are congenial for the development of disease (Siddaramaiah and Hedge, 1989). It reduces about 10-20 per cent of leaf yield depending on the season and variety of the mulberry. In addition, the infected leaves used for silkworm rearing shows adverse effects on the quality of cocoons produced (Damicone *et al.*, 2002).

Pathogen and disease cycle: A fungal pathogen *Cercospora moricola* (Cooke) causes the disease. The disease was first reported on mulberry from Allahabad (Mitter and Tandon, 1937). Subsequently, the disease was reported from many other mulberry-growing areas of the country (Rangaswamy *et al.*, 1976). The fungus produces a compact mass of interwoven cushion like hyphae on which conidiophores are produced. Conidiophores are dark; fasciculate and geniculate at the point of spore production and held together in a sticky substance. Conidia are 3-7 celled, hyaline, elongate and filiform with bulbous base, colourless and tapering at one end measuring 70×30 mm in size (Sengupta *et. al.*, 1990). The conidia are capable of producing new hyphae from any cell. The conidia disperse through rainwater. The disease spreads primarily with rain droplets through conidia and takes 10-15 days after inoculation for the development of the symptoms. Environmental factors have great influence on the disease development. The disease is favoured by constant temperature around 24°C with high atmospheric humidity of 90 per cent. Moreover, irregular harvesting of leaves and closed spacing of mulberry plants favoured the outbreak of the disease.

Control Measures

Varietal resistance: Varieties such as Kaliakutai, Kosen, Balidivalia, RFS-135, RFS-175, C799, MR1, MR2, Assambola,

K2, S54 and S36 are reported to be moderately resistant to this disease. Presence of high quantity of wax on leaf has been attributed for partial resistance to C. *moricola* (Philip *et al.*, 1992 a).

Cultural control: Avoid sprinkler irrigation. Wider spacing, balanced fertilizer, field sanitation and proper weeding will reduce the disease intensity.

Biological control: Micro-organisms *viz. Streptomyces* spp., *Chladosporium cladosporioides, Curvularia lunata* are antagonistic to the pathogen which may be exploited in the integrated gardens for disease management.

Chemical control: Carbendazim (50% WP) or Benlate (Benomyl 50% WP) at 0.025-0.05 per cent conc. (Safe period – 10 days). Spraying Carbendazim has proved to be more effective when sprayed twice at 15 days intervals with a waiting period of 15 days before feeding the mulberry leaves to silkworm. Two foliar sprays with systemic fungicide, Bavistin 50 WP (0.1%) @ 500-650 g/h at an interval of 10 - 15 days reduce the leaf spot incidence with 8 days safe period.

Leaf extracts of plants such as *Allium sativum, Calotropis gigantea, Eucalyptus* sp., *Eupatorium odoratum* etc are reported to have inhibitory effect on germination of conidia of C. *moricola* (Biswas *et al.*, 1995).

***Myrothecium* leaf spot (Tar leaf spot)**: It is reported from all the three major silk producing countries of the world *viz.*, China, India and Japan.

Taxonomic Position

Order	:	Moniliales
Class	:	Deuteromycetes
Family	:	Hypocreales
Genus	:	*Myrothecium*
Species	:	*roridum* (F.)

Symptoms

- Appearance of small pinhead brown spots on both the surfaces of mulberry leaves.
- Spots gradually increase in size and produce large irregular brown necrotic spots. Small sessile circular, discoid or irregular shaped sporodochia appear on both sides of the leaves. The sporodochia develop more on lower side of the necrotic surface.
- Formation of holes due to the falling of necrotic area in the later stage.
- Severely affected leaves become yellow and wither off.
- Biochemical analysis of the infected leaves shows depletion in iron, phosphorus and potassium contents, while calcium, magnesium, manganese and sodium are increased (Kumar *et al.*, 1991).

Predisposing Factors

- The disease is air borne and spreads by conidia.
- Susceptible genotype.
- 30-35°C atmospheric temperature and 80-90 per cent Relative Humidity are most favourable for the multiplication of the pathogen.
- Closer spacing and less air permeability in mulberry garden favours the disease development.
- Frequent rain.

Seasonal incidence: The disease generally occurs during rainy season (June-Nov.) especially in the States of West Bengal, Assam, Manipur and Nagaland and its outbreak is sporadic in southern states. However, its severity is very high during July-September. It reduces about 10-15 per cent leaf production.

Pathogen and disease cycle: *Myrothecium* Leaf Spot (MLS) caused by *Myrothecium roridum* (F.) is one of the major fungal leaf spot diseases of mulberry in the Eastern and North-eastern states of India. The spots appear dark in colour. The necrotic area is greyish. Conidia are born on the lower surface of the leaves. They are born on shield shaped white structure called sporodochia. Sporodochia are sessile, discoid and polymorphic in surface view. Conidiophores are unbranched, 30-40 mm long and 2 mm wide. Conidia are cylindrical, truncated at both ends, smoky or olive green in colour. The conidia disperse through rainwater. Contaminated soil and infected plant debris are the major sources of inoculum. The pathogen remains active in temperature range of 10-30°C with optimum of 28°C (Reming *et al.*, 1988). The pathogen remains in saprophytic conditions in soil with the capability to become pathogenic under favourable conditions. The conidia formed under warm and humid climates infect the host tissue on which fungal multiplication occurs. Thereafter, secondary infections are caused by the conidia producing on the host surface, repeatedly.

Control Measures

Varietal resistance: No variety is completely resistant to the disease. However varieties *viz.* S799 and C1729 are moderately resistant.

Cultural control: Avoid sprinkler irrigation. Wider spacing, proper weeding, thorough digging and cleaning plant debris in which pathogen harbours will reduce the disease intensity considerably.

Chemical control: Foliar spray of 0.1 per cent Carbendazim 50WP (Bavistin)—a systematic fungicide (2 gm/litre of water) at early stages of infection. Recommended fungicide solution should be sprayed when disease symptoms are noticed. Spray may be repeated after 10 days, if required. Leaves should be fed to silkworms after 7 days of spray.

(*b*) MINOR DISEASES

(*i*) **Brown spot** (*Phloeospora* **leaf spot)**: Brown spot also known as '*Phloeospora* leaf spot' occurs in almost all Sericultural countries. It causes great reduction in leaf yield due to defoliation of infected leaves.

Taxonomic Position

Order	:	Pezizomycotina
Class	:	Ascomycetes
Family	:	Ascomycetidae
Genus	:	*Phloeospora*
Species	:	*maculans* (W.)

Causal organism: *Phloeospora maculans* W. (*Septogloeum mori, Mycosphaerella mori*) is the causal agent of the disease. The disease was reported by Munshi *et al*. (1986) from Kashmir valley.

Symptoms

- Infection commences on both surfaces of leaves as minutes circular dots, which later turn grayish white in the center surrounded by a broad yellow diffusion zone.
- In wet season, the necrotic portion of the spot is rotted away and the leaves become perforated, while in dry season, the centre is split open.
- The spots at maturity become reddish gray.

Seasonal incidence: In India, the disease is very common in Kashmir, where it appears more during rainy - autumn (June-October) seasons.

Disease cycle: The pathogen over winters in the form of pseudothecia or conidia on leaves and twigs remaining attached to mulberry tree or on decomposed organic matters in soil. Over wintered conidia cause the first infection with the help of wind and rain. It takes 10 days for re-infection. A lot of re-infection occurs during favourable conditions within a short period.

Predisposing factors: The disease is air borne and spreads through conidia. High temperature and humidity, especially, high humidity is the key factor for wide spread of the disease. Therefore, any wet condition in mulberry field cause high disease incidence. Occurrence of disease has close relation with host resistance.

Control Measures

- Field sanitation by elimination of weeds and infected fallen leaves and burning them properly.
- Plantation of resistant cultivars.
- Spray of 0.05 to 0.1 per cent Bavistin or Captan (0.4%) for effective control of the fungus.

(ii) Fusarium leaf blight: The disease occurs all over India, however, in Karnataka, its incidence is very significant. It is generally known as 'leaf blight' in South India while in other places, mostly as 'twig blight'.

Taxonomic Position

Order	:	Moniliales
Class	:	Deuteromycetes
Family	:	Moniliaceae
Genus	:	*Fusarium*
Species	:	*pallidoroseum* (Cooke)

Causal organism: The disease is caused by *Fusarium pallidoroseum* (Cooke), *F. lateritium* (Nees), *F. moniliformae, F. solani* (Mart.).

Disease cycle: From fungal hyphae, simple conidiophores grow on the leaf surface in clusters. Conidiophores produce micro and macro conidia. Microconidia are single celled and ovoid or oblong in shape, while macro conidia are hyaline, elongate, filiform and multiseptate with pointed ends. Each macro conidium give rise one to several germ tubes which grow towards the stomata and penetrate the mulberry leaf through stomata.

Symptoms

- Marginal browning of leaves and formation of irregular black lesion at the initial stage of infection, which at later stage coalesces and spread longitudinally resulting in splitting and drying of branches. The branches become feeble and fragile (Govindaiah *et al.*, 1990).
- The spores germinate fairly well in day environment enabling the pathogen to cause problems in dry soil.

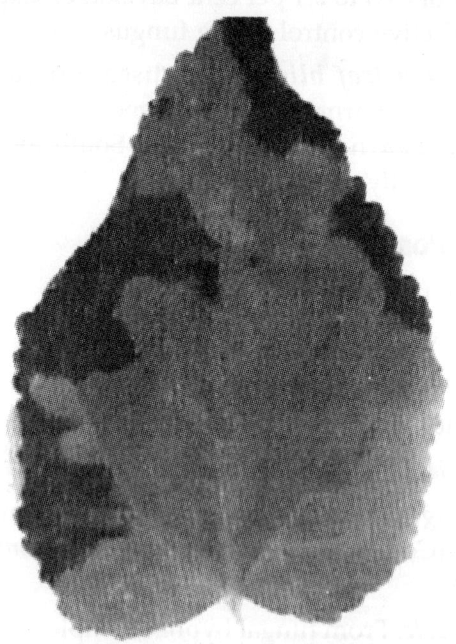

***Fusarium* leaf blight**

Seasonal incidence: The disease prevails throughout the year with a peak in summer and rainy seasons and causes 5-8 per cent leaf yield loss (Latha *et al.,* 1993).

Control Measures

- Spraying of 0.2 per cent Dithane M-45.
- Foltaf at 0.2 per cent concentration has shown complete inhibition of fungal growth (Govindaiah *et al.,* 1990 c).
- *Trichoderma* can be used as biocontrol agent against the pathogen (Latha *et al.,* 1993).
- Application of bio-fertilizers along with NPK for well nourishment of mulberry plants also reduces disease incidence (Sharma *et al.,* 1995).

(*iii*) Fusarium Leaf Spot

Causal organism: The disease is caused by *Fusarium concolor* (Reinking) and *Fusarium solani* (Mart.). Reddy and Rao (1974) reported the occurrence of *F. concolor* from Chittor district of Andhra Pradesh.

Taxonomic Position

Order	:	Moniliales
Class	:	Deuteromycetes
Family	:	Moniliaceae
Genus	:	*Fusarium*
Species	:	*Solani (Mart.)*

Symptoms

- Numerous scattered, sharply defined, brownish necrotic spots of 1-3 mm diameters appear on the infected leaves.
- Infected leaves become chlortic and fall prematurely.
- It reduces leaf production to the extent of 5-8 per cent.

- The mycelia of the fungus are floccose and whitish to incarnate or orange.

Seasonal incidence: The leaf spot disease caused by fungus is found to occur during winter season.

Pathogenic Factor

- The disease is air borne and spreads by conidia.
- Temperature of 25-32°C and below 70 per cent relative humidity favours disease development.

Fusarium **leaf spot**

(iv) Alternaria leaf blight: The disease manifests on leaf of both established and young mulberry plants, particularly by seedling stage.

Taxonomic Position

Order	:	Moniliales
Class	:	Deuteromycetes
Family	:	Dematiaceae

Genus : *Alternaria*

Species : *alternata* (Fr.)

Causal organism: The disease is caused by *Alternaria alternata* (Fr.). It can easily be identified by morphology of their large conidia. Conidiophores and conidia are yellowish in colour. Temperature ranging 28-30°C favors the multiplication of fungus.

Symptoms

- It manifests by the appearance of slight burning of leaf tips.
- Brownish, smooth and irregular concentric rings encircled by hollow margin.
- Infected leaves dry up and saplings die after few days.
- In severe cases leaves become yellow, wither and fall-off.
- Seedlings are found to be more vulnerable and dried with 10-15 days of infection.

Seasonal incidence: Causing average damage of seedlings in nurseries during October-November in Karnataka (Gunasekhar *et al.*, 1992).

Disease cycle: The pathogen is a weak parasite, which forms black or red coloured colonies. Conidiophores are simple, smooth, 1-3 septate, measuring 3-5 m × 24-60 mm with a pore at the apex. Conidia are smooth and formed in long chains. Conidia germinate by producing more than one germ tubes which terminate to form finger like projections known as appressoria. These appressoria help the pathogen to enter the leaf tissues by either direct penetration through leaf cuticle and epidermis or through wounds (Gupta *et al.*, 1998). The pathogen remains dormant in infected leaves and survives in soil and can infest new crop when the condition is favourable. The spores formed during favourable conditions infect host plants both by direct and stomatal penetration. The disease manifests on leaf within three days of fungal contact (Gunasekhar *et al.*, 1992). Re-infection occurs in plants by the spores formed in the spots.

Pathogenic factor: Abnormally high percentage of moisture in air and soil favour the disease occurrence. Seedlings are more susceptible than adult plants.

Control Measures

- Plantation of resistant mulberry varieties.
- Spraying of sensitive fungicides.

(*v*) Sooty mould

Taxonomic Position

Order	:	Ascomycota
Class	:	Meliolales
Family	:	Meliolaceae
Genus	:	*Meliola*
Species	:	*amphitricha*

Causal organism: The disease is caused by *Meliola amphitricha*.

Symptoms

- Thick dark brown to black coating develops on the upper surface of leaves, which is composed of fungal mycelia and fruiting bodies.
- The fungous grows in the secretion of insect of whitefly (*Dialeuropora decempuncta*). Photosynthetic activity of the leaf adversely affected due to black cover over the leaf, which reduces the nutritional value of leaves. The leaves also become toxic for silkworm feeding.

Seasonal incidence: The disease appears during August and continued up to December. Peak season of occurrence is during October-November.

Control Measures

- Spraying of 0.01 per cent Monocrotophos to control the Whitefly infestation.
- Spray of 0.2 per cent Indofil M-45 found effective to control the saprophytic fungi grow on the surface of the leaves.

(*vi*) Stem Blight

Causal organism: It is caused by *Phoma exigua* (Desm.).

Symptoms

- It attacks tender stems which become pale brown and swollen.
- The leaf withers off and stem break at the point of infection.
- Sub-erumpent round pycnidia of the pathogen are seen in the necrotic region.

Seasonal incidence: The stem blight disease occurs in the hills of Tamil Nadu during July-October (Yadav and Sukumar, 1987).

Disease cycle: The pathogen is a weak parasite. It forms sub-epidermal pycnidia in concentric rings. Pycnidia are globose to sub-globose or obpyriform and ostiolate. Pycnidia wall is pseudoparenchymatous to prosenchymatous, with outer cell dark and thick walled and inner cells isodiometric and hyaline. Conidiogenous cells are indistinguishable from inner cells. Conidia arise as buds in basipetal succession from the apex of conidiogenous cells, hyaline to globose to obovoidal and aseptic.

Control Measures

- The affected shoots should be cut-off early and destroyed by burning.
- The cuttings and leaf plucking should be carried out with proper care and as far as possible the injuries during these operations should be avoided.

- Land should be deeply ploughed and exposed to sunlight.
- Cutting should be soaked in 0.1 per cent Dithane M-45.
- Efforts should be made to keep away the mulberry shoot pests.
- Soil application of Nursery Guard (a bio-formulation of *Trichoderma pseudokoningii*) reduces the disease occurrence considerably.
- Application of adequate quantity of nitrogen fertilizers reduces the incidence of disease.
- Leaf extract of neem and fungicide Dithan-45 (Mancozeb 75 WP) have been found to be effective against the disease.

(*vii*) Stem canker

The disease occurs in the tropical and sub-tropical regions of India. However, its occurrence is very high the state of Karnataka especially during rainy season.

Taxonomic Position

Order	:	Coelomycetidae
Class	:	Deuteromycetes
Family	:	Melanconiales
Genus	:	*Botryodiplodia*
Species	:	*theobromae* (Pat.)

Causal organism: Stem canker caused by fungus, *Botryodiplodia theobromae* (Pat.) was first reported by Luke and Paul (1982). The fungus is wide spread in distribution and occurs in the tropical and sub-tropical warm places of India. The disease is reported to cause severe loss in the nursery killing 30-70 per cent of the cuttings (Sukumar *et al.*, 1991).

Symptoms

The initial symptoms on established plants are drying and browning of bark at the cut ends after pruning operations.

The drying extends downwards and kills buds. Occasionally withering and death of sprouting plants may also occur. Greenish black lesions appear on the stem and plenty of dark black carbonaceous structures producing pycnidial bodies in groups in later stages. It inhibits sprouting of cuttings. The pathogen invades the stem through wounds caused during preparing the cuttings or due to pruning operation.

In nurseries the first visible symptoms is the failure of the cutting to sprout. The bark rots and gets easily peeled off. Black pycnidial bodies are seen on the bark. Root initiation is inhibited and the sprouts if developed wither and die. The pycnidiospores are dispersed through wind, irrigation water and rain splash. Delayed sprouting after pruning has been found to be a major predisposing factor for pathogenic invasion.

Seasonal incidence: The disease occurs throughout the year with highest incidence during rainy season.

Control Measures

(a) Physical Control

- Removal and destruction of infected cuttings and saplings in nurseries reduces inoculums. In established gardens, the affected stem parts should be cut and burnt.
- Repeated rising of sapling in the same field should be avoided, as it helps in inoculums build-up in the soil.
- Stacking the pruned stem portions by the side of the mulberry garden should be avoided since they produce an excellent substratum for the growth and multiplication of the fungus.
- Planting during winter months should be avoided since cold weather delays normal sprouting thereby predisposing the cuttings to infection.

(b) Chemical Control

Stem cuttings should be soaked in 0.2 per cent Carbendazim solution (2 gm of chemical in one litre of water) for 20-30 minutes before planting.

- In nurseries where severe incidence of disease appeared, soil should be disinfected with Captan or Carbendazim at the rate 8 kg/acre prior to planting of cuttings (Sukumar *et al.*, 1991). After 10-12 days, well-decomposed Farm Yard Manure (FYM) should be applied and thoroughly mixed with soil for planting the cuttings. Post treatment application of FYM is a prerequisite prior to planting in treated soil.
- To prevent bud mortality on established plants, cut end should be sprayed with 0.2 per cent Carbendazim or Captan solution.

Shirata *et al.* (1979) reported 30 isolates of *Fusarium* spp. from twig blight infected mulberry shoots and classified them into *F. lateritium; F. solani; F. roseum* and *F. moniliformae.*

(c) Biological Control

Nursery Guard, a bio-formulation of *Trochoderma pseudokoningii* can be used for long-term protection, better survival and growth of saplings. Mix 1 kg of Nursery Guard with 60 kg of finely powdered well decomposed FYM/ neem cake. Moisten the mixture to a maximum of 30 per cent moisture, store in under shade in the form of heap and cover with a wet gunny cloth. This enhances the multiplication of biological control agent in the mixture. Broadcast the mixture @2 kg/m^2 over the well prepared nursery beds and thoroughly mix with soil by light digging. Apply the mixture only to the planting area in nursery beds.

(*viii*) Root Rots Diseases

Root rot is the most dangerous disease due to its epidemic nature and potentiality to kill the plants completely poses a serious threat to mulberry in almost all the sericultural countries. Various types of mulberry root rot diseases have been reported from all over the world. These are dry root rot, white root rot, *Armilaria* root rot, violet root rot, black root rot, charcoal root rot and bacterial root rot. Among them, the dry (*Fusarium*), black and charcoal root rots are reported in India (Sukumar and Padma, 1999). The disease was reported from almost all types of soils under varied agro-climatic conditions throughout the year. It initially appears in an isolated patch in few plants, which act as a centre for the spread of the disease leading to the death of the plants within a short period.

White root rot: The disease mainly occurs in temperate places.

Taxonomic Position

Phylum	:	Ascomyceta
Class	:	Ascomycetes
Order	:	Xylariales
Family	:	Xylariaceae
Genus	:	*Rosellinia*
Species	:	*necatrix* (Berl.)

Causal organism: The disease is caused by *Rosellinia necatrix* (Berl). It is very common and found throughout India.

Symptoms

- Affected plants show stunted growth and yellowing of leaves.
- White velvet like mycelia mat spread on stem and roots.
- The diseased mulberry plants become very weak, the leaf buds grow feebly, leaves wither off and plant dies very soon.

The fungus over winters in the form of hyphal strands, sclerotic and rhizomorph on the diseased roots along with root stumps in the soil. It reproduces asexually by chlamydospores, sclerotia and rarely through conidia while sexual reproduction takes place by asci and ascospores in closed fruiting body called perithecium. Each ascus has 8 ascospores, which are dark brown and spindle shaped. Ascospore germinates under favourable conditions and infects the root system. The fungus can survive in the soil up to a depth of 100 cm for 4-5 years. Soil temperature 25-30°C with more than 70 per cent humidity is favourable for disease development (Ertian, 2003). Presence of plant debris in field increases disease spread.

Seasonal incidence: It causes extensive damage to mulberry field by killing the well-established plants especially during summer.

Control Measure

- The diseased soil is to be fumigated with chloropicrin or calcium cynamide at 1 pound per 108 sq. ft. or 75 gm per 36 sq. ft. respectively.
- The diseased seedlings should not be used for planting and after disinfections the seedling should be immersed in hot water at about 45°C and kept for 60 minutes, whereby the fungi are completely destroyed.
- The diseased stumps should be removed rapidly and the location of the stumps should be treated with chloropicrin.
- Keep the plants well nourished.

Violet root rot: The violet root rot disease of mulberry occurs widely in China, Japan, Korea, Thailand and Vietnam.

Taxonomic Position

Phylum	:	Basidiomycota
Class	:	Ustilaginomycetes

Order	:	Platygloeales
Family	:	Platygloeaceae
Genus	:	*Helicobasidium*
Species	:	*mompa* (Tanaka)

Causal organism: It is caused by *Helicobasidium mompa* (Tanaka), which causes considerable damage by attacking the mulberry roots.

Symptoms

- Violet colored velvet like mycelial mat spreads on stem and roots.
- Infected root rots and thread like rhizomorphs are visible on roots.
- Infected stems wither.
- Sudden withering off of leaves takes place followed by decay and dying of the plant in severe cases.
- The epidermal tissues of the roots are covered with whitish violet coloured mycelial mat.
- The affected plants or stumps lose hold on the soil and can be uprooted easily with very little effort.
- Only the un-rotten xylem exists in the uprooted root.

Seasonal incidence: It is more prevalent in waterlogged areas throughout the year.

Pathogen and disease cycle: Mycelia are both vegetative and reproductive. Vegetative mycelia are yellowish brown, 5-10 μ in diameter and amoeboid in shape. Reproductive mycelia forms loose floccose purplish brown basidicarp with more or less interwoven hyphae of 5-6 μ diameter. Basidiospores are colourless, smooth and oval to elongated oval with one end curve. Sclerotia are semi-round, violet-red and formed on the surface of decayed root. The fungus lives parasitically on mulberry root or saprophytic ally on the organic matters in soil. During favourable season, the vegetative mycelia or sclerotia produce new hyphae, which enter through the lenticels of new roots and gradually spread towards the lateral and main roots. Abundant hyphae are developed in cortex surrounding the xylem and cause severe degeneration of the cortex cells. In rainy season, the pathogen forms basidia with basidiospores. The basidiospores germinate into hyphae but they have no infection ability and finally die.

Control Measures

- Inter cropping of susceptible crops in mulberry fields should be avoided.
- Cultivate graminaceous crop for 3-4 years as rotation crop in the infected area.
- Saplings should be disinfected with 0.2 per cent Bavistin powder for 30 minutes at 45°C or 0.3 per cent Bleaching powder for 30 minutes.
- 30 cm×30 cm×30 cm pits should be prepared at a distance of 3 meters. Disinfection of soil with 150-200 gm of Chloropicrin or Calcium cynamide/meter square is recommended to control the violet root rot disease.
- Saplings selected for cultivation should be prepared in areas free from the occurrence of this infection. They should also be checked to confirm the absence of mycelial strands on them.
- The damaged stocks should be uprooted and destroyed by burning. The soil should be treated with 2 per cent formalin solution.
- Soils should be well manure and the plants must be healthy in all aspects to increase their disease resistance.
- Application of sodium nitrate in the soil controls the spread of the disease. Lime also suppresses the growth of the pathogen.
- It is also effective to prevent the spreading of this disease by digging trenches around the mulberry fields.

Collar rot: The disease is common in mulberry and found to occur in Karnataka during the months of July-September. The disease is favoured by high soil moisture contents.

Causal organism: It is caused by *Phoma mororum* (Sacc.) and is common in rainy season. The disease was first reported from Tamil Nadu (Yadav and Sukumar, 1987).

Symptoms

- The infected stem discolors at ground level and the leaves whither.
- White mycelium mat develops at the infection site, which later produces sub erumpent dark pycnidia causing wilting of plants.

Control Measures

- Land should be deeply ploughed and exposed to sunlight.
- Cutting should be soaked in 0.1 per cent Dithane M-45.
- Soil application of Nursery guard (a bio-formulation of *Trichoderma pseudokoningii*).

Black Root Rot (DieBack)

Taxonomic Position

Order	:	Sphaeropsitales
Class	:	Deuteromycetes
Family	:	Sphaeropsidaceae
Genus	:	*Botryodiplodia*
Species	:	*theobromae* (Pat.)

The disease is caused by *Lasiodiplodia (Botryodiplodia) theobromae* (Sukumar *et al.*, 1994; Radhakrishnan *et al.*, 1995). The disease is prevalent throughout Karnataka and Tamil Nadu.

Symptoms

- Infected plants show sudden wilting, defoliation of leaves and finally death of plant.
- Infected plants show maceration and collapse of tissues.
- Rotting and peeling of bark exposing wood enveloped by grayish black mycelium on mature roots while total rotting of all the tissues in case of tender roots. The rotting and peeling of bark sometimes extends up to the stem region near the soil line.

The pathogen enters the host through cut ends of the stem after pruning. The fungus prefers 25-30°C for good growth and does not survive at above/beyond 40°C. The pathogen survives on all types of substrate such as soil, weeds debris and stacked mulberry twigs. Once the plants are vulnerable to infection, the fungus dominates inside the roots multiplying the hyphae rapidly in the cortical tissues and extending up to the pith. It enters the xylem vessels and causes death of the plant.

Seasonal incidence: It occurs from April-November.

Control Measures

- Pruning and destruction of infected twigs.
- Spray of 0.2 per cent Carbendazim or Captan to the stumps after pruning.
- Foe better result spray of fungicide @ 8 kg/acre combined with soil. Soil application should be given after 10 days of aerial spray (Sukumar *et al.*, 2000).

Dry (*Fusarium*) Root Rot

Root rot is one of the dangerous diseases of mulberry as it kills the plant completely. The disease has become more alarming due to its endemic and soil borne nature. The disease is generally observed at severe under water stress conditions as well as soil with poor organic contents.

Taxonomic Position

Order	:	Moniales
Class	:	Deuteromycetes
Family	:	Tuberculariaceae
Genus	:	Fusarium
Species	:	*solani* (Mart.)

Causal Organism: Various pathogenic fungi such as *Fusarium solani* (Mart.), *Fusarium oxysporum* and *Botryodiplodia theobomae,* etc. have been found associated with mulberry under different agro-climatic conditions. Species of *Fusarium* occur usually in many crop plants including mulberry throughout the world and dominates in tropical zones.

Symptoms

- Drooping of leaf petiole.
- Sudden wilting/withering and defoliation of leaves followed by drying/death of affected leaves. Withering and defoliation start from bottom of the branch and progress upwards.
- Decaying of root bark and roots. Due to this mulberry leaves become yellow and drooping of foliage takes place before extensive wilting.
- The leaves showed withering symptoms when most of the roots are decayed. In severe cases, the entire root system gets decayed and plants die.
- Affected plants after pruning either fail to sprout or when the plants sprout bear small and pale yellow leaves with rough surface. The severely affected plants loose hold in soil and can easily be uprooted.

The disease spreads fast primarily through contaminated soil, farm implements and irrigation. The secondary source of infestation is through diseased saplings (Philip *et al.,* 1996).

The species of *Fusarium* invades mostly the roots through wounds caused by mechanical injuries. The fungus produces numerous micro and macro conidia and chlymydospores, which are characteristics of the genus. The micro conidia are small sickle shaped and multiseptate while macro conidia are oval shaped. *Fusarium* can live in soil saprophytically and survives for 5-6 years. *Fusarium* secretes proteolytic enzymes, which partly destroy the middle lamellae of xylem parenchyma and degrade pectic compounds in the walls of xylem vessels and trachides. Due to the infection, the parenchymatous cells are killed which turn brown to blackish in colour.

Control Measures

- Good hygienic condition and sanitation at field are the best measures to avoid the problems of root rot disease.
- Apply more quantity of organic manures such as Farm Yard Manure (FYM), compost, green manure, press mud etc. in affected areas.
- The infested land should be deep ploughed and the soil should be exposed to sunlight during summer months to kill the pathogens.
- Dead plants should be uprooted and burnt immediately. The uprooted area should be heated by burning dry leaves and grasses.
- Intercropping of various crop plants such as beans, onion, sesame, sorghum, etc., is found to reduce the incidence of root rot disease.
- Crop rotation may also help to slow down the build up of the inoculums load of root rot pathogens and prevent them from reaching destructive level.
- Dithane M-45 @ 5-10 gm/plant after removing the soil around the infected plant to a depth of 5-6″ and irrigation reduces the incidence of disease. Subsequently, after one month apply Raksha (a bio-formulation of *Trichoderma harzianum*) @ 500 gm/plant after removing

soil around the infected plant. To prepare the Raksha mixture, mix 1 kg Raksha with 50 kg FYM/neem cake (sufficient for 100 plants) and keep under shade for a week to enhance the multiplication of *Trichoderma* colony. About 25-30 per cent moisture should be maintained by sprinkling water. The application of Raksha can be given 4 times a year at an interval of 3 months.

Integrated method to control the disease is most effective. This method involves the combined application of Dithane M-45 and a bio-fungicide named as Raksha produced by *Trichoderma harzianum* (Sharma, 1999b). In integrated method, Dithan-45 reduces the pathogen load in soil whereas *T. harzianum* is inhibiting the growth of pathogen by various types of phenomena such as hyper parasitism, competition and antibiosis. During antibiosis, the antagonist is also known to produce chitanases. Trichodermin and gluconase dissolves the cell wall of the pathogenic fungi or arrest the growth (Tronsmo, 1996).

Charcoal rot: The charcoal rot disease is also known as 'ashy stem blight'. In India, the disease occurs in nursery beds of mulberry and affects the plant mostly at its seedling stage.

Taxonomic Position

Order	:	Spheropsidales
Class	:	Deuteromycetes
Family	:	Sphaeropsidaceae
Genus	:	*Macrophomina*
Species	:	*phaseolina* (Tassi)

Causal organism: Charcoal rot is caused by a pathogen *Macrophomina phaseolina* (Tassi). In India, the disease is observed in various parts of Tamil Nadu. The occurrence of this disease at present is marginal.

Symptoms

- The disease symptoms start from yellowing of leaves followed by drooping of branches.
- The affected roots are brown turning black like charcoal and tissues become weak breaking off easily.
- In severe cases, the sclerotial bodies are seen scattered on the affected root tissues.
- The affected plants fail to sprout after pruning and dry up completely (Sridhar *et al.*, 2000; Choudhary *et al.*, 2003).

Control Measures

- Field sanitation practices and protective chemical spray in soil helps to reduce the disease intensity.
- Antagonistic microbs (*Bacillus subtillis*) with inhibitory effect against *M. phaseolina* can be utilized to control the disease (Sridhar *et al.*, 2000).

Stem Rots (*Sclerotium rolfsii* - Sacc.)

The pathogen is a soil borne fungus, living saprophytically on dead plant debris. It is a weak pathogen that becomes active in the presence of host under favourable conditions. As this fungus requires warm and humid conditions for its active growth and perpetuation, the pathogen after remaining dormant inside the bark or in the soil becomes active with monsoon showers and multiplies rapidly, producing sporangia and zoospores for secondary spread.

Causal organism: The disease was reported on mulberry from Dharwad by Siddaramaiah and Patil (1984) and from Bangalore by Yadav and Kasturibai (1988). The disease appears sporadic, assumes epidemic proportions in the fairly grown plants also, particularly after early monsoon showers, which provide congenial weather conditions for the growth and multiplication of disease causing pathogen. It is caused by *Sclerotium rolfsii*. The fungus survives in soil and in infected plant debris/stubbles. Under congenial conditions, the fungal spores germinate and invade the host plant.

Symptoms

- The infection is mostly confined to basal portion of the stem and under severe conditions; it infects upper parts of the stem and branches.
- Wilting of sprouted cuttings and leaf scorching.
- Dark brown to black water soaked spots on the collar region of the stem, which rapidly encircle the stem.
- The characteristics feature of the disease is development of white mycelial mat with chocolate brown sclerotial bodies over infected tissue.
- Sclerotic ellipsoidal in shape and vary from 0.5-1.5 mm in size.
- At advanced stages, the leaves fall down at a slight touch and plants wilt completely.

Control Measures

- Preparation of cuttings for propagation only from healthy plants.
- Adoption of field sanitation practices.
- Application of sufficient amount of well decomposed organic manure in the soil to encourage antagonistic microbial population.
- Removal of diseased and dead plants and their appropriate disposal by burning etc, to prevent secondary spread of disease.
- Pruning of stem at 30 cm above ground level.
- Drenching soil with Bavistin (0.10%), Brassicol (0.2%) or Captan (0.2%)).
- Integrated control with nitrogen fertilizers and *Trichoderma hazarianum*.

(2) Bacterial Diseases: Several bacterial diseases often affect mulberry plants, but amongst them, bacterial blight is the major prevalent one.

(*i*) Bacterial blight (*Pseudomonas mori*)

Taxonomic Position

Order	:	Pseudomonadales
Class	:	Schizomycetes
Family	:	Psedomonadaceae
Genus	:	*Pseudomonas*
Species	:	*mori* (Boyer and Lambart)

Symptoms

- General die back of twigs and stunted growth of young trees.
- Small, irregular shaped brown to black spots surrounded by yellow halo develop on the lamina and veins of the leaves on the lower surface, which later appear on the upper leaf surface.
- Infected leaves curl, roll up and fall off.
- Elongated ragged lesions appear on the young shoots.
- Besides defoliation, the disease impairs the nutritive value of mulberry leaves making unsuitable for silkworm rearing.
- Young leaves are more susceptible than mature ones, which get crinkled, distorted, curved outward and drop prematurely.

Seasonal incidence: It is a serious disease in India and cause 5-10 per cent leaf yield loss (Teotia and Sen, 1993) during rainy season (June-October). The disease is more severe in mulberry grown under tropical conditions.

Pathogen and disease cycle: The disease is caused by *Pseudomonas mori* (Boyer and Lambart). The disease was first reported from Nainital (Sinha and Saxena, 1966) and subsequently from almost all mulberry-growing areas of India (Prasad and Siddaramaiah, 1978; Teotia and Sen, 1994; Gunasekhar *et al.*, 1994; Maji and Quadri, 1999). Soil is the primary source of bacterial inoculums. The secondary infection of the disease takes place through irrigation, cultivation activities, mechanical injuries and biological agents. The bacterium is rod shaped, non-motile, gram negative, encapsulated with no endospore. Infection occurs from the bacteria exuding from the shoot lesions during rain, which washed them over the surface to bring about further infection. Infected leaves turn yellow, curl and fall off. The bacterium is rod shaped, measuring 0.-1.4 µm by 1.8-4.5 µm. It is mainly characterized by small circular shiny white translucent slow growing colonies. Bacteria over winters in their natural ooze or other plant parts fallen on the soil for 3-4 months. On living plants, they survive epiphytically in buds, on wounds, in exudates or inside the infected tissues. Penetrating bacteria are carried to the infection site (stomata, hydathodes, wounds etc) by rain splash, insects or by wind during wet weather. After landing on wet leaves, they multiply in a film of water and penetrate through stomata, hydathodes or wounds caused by insects or mechanical injuries. Inside the tissue, they multiply and spread intercellular at a rapid rate.

Predisposing factors: Regular rain, high humidity, moderate temperature, dense planting, neglected care favour the development of the disease. Low temperature and dry whether prolong the survival of the bacteria. Presence of dead mulberry leaves and twigs in soil also favours pathogen to survive long.

Control Measures

- Affected plants should be uprooted, removed and burnt.
- The contaminated soil should be exposed for sun drying.

- Tilling and levelling of soil at the stump area.
- Use of bio-fertilizers, Azospirillium, Azotobacter and VAM are able to minimize disease incidence (Sharma *et al.*, 2000).
- Streptocycline solution (1 gm of the chemical in 100 litres of water) as foliar spray twice at 4 days interval has been found effective.
- Pruning of minor infected shoot followed by spray with Borax mixture.
- Spraying of Foltaf followed by Mancozeb and Captan at 0.25 per cent is also effective against the pathogen (Sharma and Govindaiah, 1991).
- Varieties such as Kajali, MR2, Mysore Local, S36 and S54 are reported to be moderately resistant to *P. mori* (Shree and Boraiah, 1988).

(*ii*) Bacterial leaf spot

Taxonomic Position

Order	:	Pseudomonadales
Class	:	Schizomycetes
Family	:	Pseudomonadaceae
Genus	:	*Xanthomonas*
Species	:	*campestris* (Pommel).

Symptoms

- Appearance of numerous small angular water soaked spots on lower surface of leaves which later turn brownish surrounded by yellow margin.
- Necrotic spots shed off and produce minute holes in the leaves.
- The young infected leaves curl outward and distorted. Highly infected leaves turn yellowish and falls prematurely (Maji and Quadri, 1999).

Seasonal incidence: It is a very common mulberry disease during rainy and winter season (June-October) in Karnataka, West Bengal, Uttarakhand and Orissa but maximum severity is reported during July-September. The disease starts progressing from 35th day after pruning/leaf harvest and becomes severe after 70th day.

Bacterial leaf spot

Pathogen and disease cycle: The disease is caused by *Xanthomonas campestris* (Pommel) (Maji *et al.*, 1996). It affects leaf yield of mulberry and reduce nutritional value of the leaves. Pandey and Singh (1989) reported the occurrence of disease from Dehradun (Uttaranchal). The disease causing bacterium is rod shaped with single polar flagellum, motile, occurring singly or in pairs, gram negative and encapsulated. It grows intercellular in leaf tissues and stem. Spread of the disease occurs through rain droplets and mechanical injury. It reduces leaf production up to 12 per cent.

Predisposing factors: High humidity (85-95%), temperature (30-35°C), regular rain and overdose of nitrogenous fertilizer favour the development of the disease.

Control measures: It is difficult to completely exterminate of the bacteria. However, following measures will be effective to avoid the infection to a great extent.

Cultural control: Infected leaves and branches should be cut at an early stage and destroyed by burning. Field sanitation, exposure of soil to sunlight, wider spacing and prevention from mechanical injury of leaves can reduce the disease incidence. The mulberry field management, particularly leaf plucking should be carried out carefully and plants must be well protected from possible injuries. Waste shoots must not be left in the inter-ridge spaces and at the same time dense planting should be avoided.

Chemical control: Excessive application of nitrogen fertilizer should be avoided. Spraying of agricultural antibiotics *viz.* Streptomycin or Agrimycin, Pushamycin, Plantomycin at 100 ppm concentration is reported to reduce the disease incidence (Pandey and Singh, 1989).

Varietals resistance: High yielding disease resistant varieties of mulberry namely S146, S799, S1635, V1 and MR_2 should be selected and cultivated.

***(iii)* Bacterial wilt/bacterial root rot:** This disease is typical bacterial disease infecting the vascular tracts of mulberry plants. It is very destructive and spreads with great rapidity.

Taxonomic Position

Order	:	Pseudomonadales
Class	:	Schizomycetes
Family	:	Pseudomonadaceae
Genus	:	*Pseudomonas*
Species	:	*solanacearum* (Smith)

Symptoms

The bacterium affects the roots, young seedlings and saplings leading to wilting of shoots. The disease plants shows wilting of leaves due to loss of water. Two types are wilting are developed on the aerial part. In one type, the leaves of whole branch completely loss luster and wilt very soon. Thus, the wilted leaves maintain green colours and known as 'green wilt'. In another type, the tips and margin of the leaves arising from the middle portion of one or two branches wilt and subsequently become brown, and finally, all leaves of diseased plants show similar wilting. In advanced stage, the affected region of the bark becomes black and rotten, which eventually fell off. White dirty substance also comes out from the cut end of the infected root.

Seasonal incidence: The disease commonly occurs during rainy season (April-November).

Pathogen and disease cycle: The disease is very destructive and spread rapidly and damages the whole field. The pathogen of the disease is *Pseudomonas solanacearum* (Smith). It belongs to category Pseudo single-cell bacillus. Bacterial wilt erupts generally where mulberry plants grow in abundance, more so where the disease already exists. Mathew *et al.* (1994) reported the disease from Kerala (India), but so far not assumed greater economic importance. The pathogen is soil inhabitant and survives for several years. Soil and diseased mulberry plants and other host plants are the primary source of inoculums. The pathogen disseminates by rain, irrigation water and farm implements. The bacterium is small, rod shaped, without spore and capsule, 0.8-1.9 μm in length, gram-negative and motile with 1-3 polar flagella at each end. Bacterial colony is round, smooth, shiny, moist and grayish-white at first turning black brown later. This is the result of water soluble pigment secreted by the bacteria. When the culture medium turns brown, the bacteria lose its pathogenicity. The pathogenic bacteria of bacterial wilt over winters in the diseased roots, diseased branches, damaged body of the stems and soils. The disease is soil inhabitant and can remain in particular soil for several years. Soil and diseased mulberry plants and other host plants in contaminated areas are the primary source of inoculums. Once the disease is established in an area, the pathogen will be disseminated by rain, irrigation water, cultivation etc.

Predisposing factor: High temperature, soil moisture, water logged land favour the spread the disease. The bacteria can grow in pH of 5-9 but growth is best at pH 6-8. Newly planted saplings and young mulberry plants are easily affected by the disease and perish quickly, while the older ones, which have the ability to grow new roots, can survive for a few more years as weak and in dwarf conditions.

Control Measures

- The affected plants should be dug out and burnt immediately.
- Formalin solution of 1:100 concentrations or 0.2 per cent bleaching powder solution should be applied to the diseased spots and vicinity as disinfectant.
- Cereals crop, potato, sugarcane etc should be used as rotation crops in the infected plots.
- Intercropping with wilt disease susceptible plants like tomato, cowpea, broad beans etc should be avoided as it increases disease incidence markedly.

(3) VIRAL DISEASES

(i) Mosaic disease: Mosaic virus causes it. The disease is mostly observed in temperate conditions. Raychoudhuri *et al.* (1962) for the first time reported this disease from Kalimpong (West Bengal). It has been reported that the nematodes belonging to the Genus Languorous play the role of vector for the virus infection. Survival period of the parasite is between 1-3 years. The disease is of less importance in sericulture industry, as it does not cause any economic damage in mulberry leaf production.

Symptoms

- The symptom of the disease is inward curling of leaves particularly leaf margin and tip with chlorotic lesions on the leaf surface. Significant reduction in total chlorophyll and starch contents and increase in total sugar and phenols have been reported in diseased leaves (Kumar, 1991).

- The internodes in the top portion of the shoots decrease and auxiliary buds in the upper and middle portion of the shoots takes longer period to sprout, and form small double branches with small deformed leaves.
- When the disease is severe, disease leaves roll upwards and shrinks, surface roughens, leaf blades and leaf veins turn brown, the lesions are more distinct, branches becomes thin and small, auxiliary buds develop early, side branches come up and the disease plants is easily frostbitten.
- The affected shoots in general can easily break off and die.

It is reported that the mulberry mosaic disease gradually spreads from a part of a single stump to other shoots and branches. The disease occurs irregularly in different areas of the mulberry field. Due to the occurrence of this disease, the uptake of nitrogen and phosphate by the soil decreases. This disease has not been found to spread through insect vectors.

Seasonal incidence: The disease is reported to occur throughout the year in mulberry growing areas.

Control Measures

- Disease-free mulberry seedlings and resistant cultivars should only be planted.
- Diseased plants should be removed, uprooted and burnt and the ground in these spots should be disinfected with Chloropicrin.
- Spraying of insecticides eliminate insect vectors.

(ii) Yellow net vein disease: The disease is caused by a Yellow-net Vein Virus and is transmitted by pen-grafts and inarch-grafts (Raychaudhury and Nariani, 1977). It is also transmitted through a species of white fly (*Bemisia* sp.). Raychaudhury *et al.* (1961) for the first time reported this viral disease from Kalimpong (West Bengal) and subsequently, the disease was reported from Jammu by Koul *et al.* (1991).

Symptoms

- Chlorotic area starting from margins of infected leaves. Subsequently these areas spread to the whole leaf.
- Vein and veinlets become completely yellow and give the leaf a net like appearance.
- Wedge, root and bud grafting transmit the disease.
- An average reduction of 2.3 per cent dry matter has been reported (Koul *et al.*, 1991) in affected leaves.

Control Measures

- Use virus free cutting for propagation.
- Diseased plants should be uprooted and removed.

(4) MYCOPLASMA DISEASE/DWARF DISEASE

This is very common disease in China, Japan, Korea and India. The disease is caused by mycoplasma like organism (MLO). The MLO particle is pellet shaped and about 80 μm in diameter. It contains nucleoplasm and fiber like substance. Three layers of unit membranes, which are a protein membrane, a lipoid membrane and a protein membrane from inside to outside, bound it. It is also reported that the disease can be caused by complete harvesting and excessive leaf plucking, excessive application of rapid active nitrogen fertilizer, infestation of mulberry fields by pests such as grasshoppers, galls etc and mulberry fields damaged by wind and floods. The disease reduces approximately 70 per cent leaf yield during its epidemic condition. Silkworm fed on the diseased leaves produce dull cocoons of irregular shape.

Symptoms

- The infected plants become extremely stunted. Leaves of infected plants crumpled and become extremely small, shrunken and lose green colour, comparatively yellowish and lacks glossy appearance.
- In the final stage of the disease, which is also known as severe dwarf condition, the shoots become extremely slender and small.
- Internodes become shortened.
- The plants lose vitality and die after two to three years of infection.
- The growth of vascular bundle is poor for the root, twigs and leaves. The vessel becomes thin and the number of vessels also decreases. Because of defective conductive tissues, the plants have low root pressure, weak transpiration and retention of assimilatory starch in the mesophyll of leaves.
- The cell wall becomes thin.
- The disease is considered to be one of the infectious diseases carried by Rhombic-marked leafhoppers (*Hishimonas sellatus*).

Disease cycle: The primary source of inoculums is the affected plants in fields and the vegetative propagating material *viz.*, saplings, scions, stocks and cuttings. The disease is transmitted by leafhopper (*H. sellatus*). After an incubation period of 13 days, the insect transmits the disease. Only the adult insect can transmit the disease and that efficiency remains throughout its life. Therefore, even the vector insect, which acquires them in 1st instar, will not transmit the disease until it reaches its adult stage. Apart from the vectors, the disease also spreads by means of vegetative propagation materials like, saplings, scions, stocks and cuttings, but never spreads through seeds and soil.

Control Measures

- Diseased plants should be removed and destroyed immediately on the appearance of the first symptoms.
- To grow disease-free seedlings of resistant varieties of mulberry.
- Excessive shoot cut should be avoided.
- Dig out diseased stumps, remove and discard them.
- Saplings must be quarantined before being transported.
- Pruning of plants should be carried out at higher levels.
- Improve quality of soil by application of manure.
- Avoid too much application of rapid acting nitrogen fertilizer.
- Apply higher quantity of potassium fertilizers.
- Improve the conditions of micro-contents in the soil.
- Insect vector should be prevented and controlled.
- Spraying of 0.1 gm solution of boric acid and 1.0 gm of ammonium molybdenate per mulberry stump is effective in preventing the occurrence of the disease.
- Spray of insecticides *viz.* Cidial at 1: 1000.
- Spraying of 100-ppm solution of Tetracycline hypochloride for 15 times at an interval of 2-3 days after summer pruning suppresses the disease development.

(5) ROOT KNOT/NEMATODE DISEASE

More than 42 species of nematodes belonging to 24 genera are reported to cause different diseases in mulberry all over the world. These nematodes damage mulberry plants by feeding or extraction of food from the host with the help of style and by mechanical destruction of host cells. But, more important damage they cause due to the action of esophageal secretions and enzymes which bring about disease symptoms, such as necrosis, stubby root, gall formation, distortion of growth or loss in vigor. Affected plants continue to survive as weak ones with reduced health and vigor and yielding far below of its potential.

Among nematodes, *Meloidogyne incognita* (Kofoid & White) causing root knot disease is very serious and chronic to mulberry. It occurs worldwide and ranks high in economic importance. The disease in India was first reported from Karnataka by Narayanan *et al.* (1966). Maximum intensity of the nematode is reported to be during rainy season followed by summer and minimum during winter. It is important not only due to the direct damage causing to crops but also because of its role in predisposing plants to attack by other pathogens. Since the nematodes are unseen enemies of plants, the crop losses caused by them are not only in the form of reduced plant growth and yield but also in the marketable quality of the produce. Mulberry grown in sandy soils under irrigation is most affected.

M. incognita has a wide range of host plants, which infects more than 2000 species of plants including almost all agricultural, horticultural, oil seeds, ornamental plants and plantation crops etc. *M. incognita* is more dangerous to mulberry not only because of the direct damage to the crop but also it predisposes the plant to various soil borne plant pathogens (Bhagyrathy *et al.*, 2000; Sukumar *et al.*, 2000; Nishita Naik *et al.*, 2003).

Taxonomic Position

Order	:	Tylenchida
Class	:	Secerentia
Family	:	Heteroderoidea
Genus	:	*Meloidogyne*
Species	:	*incognita* (Kofoid White)

Symptoms: In mulberry, the disease caused extensive damage due to its endoparasitic habit and perennial nature of the mulberry plant. The manifestation of disease and its effect on plant are the formation of galls/knots on the roots and stunted growth with reduced vigor of the plant (Govindaiah *et al.*, 1989; 1997). Knots are of different sizes, irregular in shape, yellowish white and with smooth surface at initial period. Later, the knots turn black and finally, they rot. Delayed sprouting after pruning, reduced leaf size, stunted growth, chlorosis and reduction in leaf yield are the other symptoms above the ground parts of the plant. Histopathological observations revealed that due to nematode infestation, the vascular tissues and cortex of roots are disorganized hampering the uptake of water and minerals from the soil to aerial parts of the plant (Ertian, 2003).

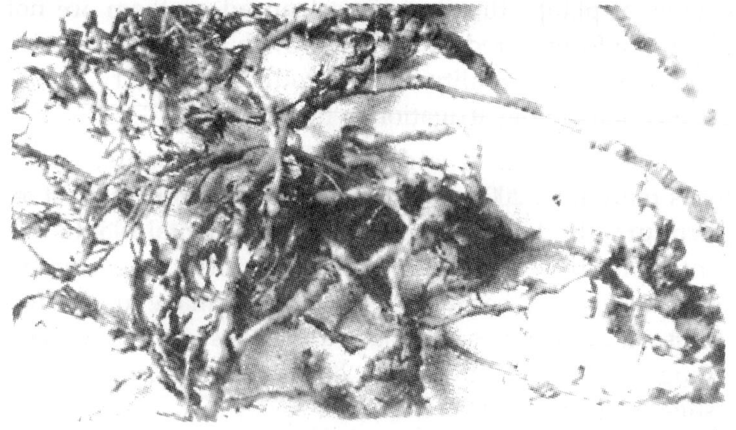

Root knot disease

Dispersal of nematode: Nematode disperses within the field and from one field to other field mainly through contaminated soil, farm machinery, sapling transplantation, run-off irrigation water etc. Cultivation of other susceptible crops along with mulberry and growth of some susceptible weeds in and around mulberry garden acts as secondary sources of infection (Govindaiah *et al.*, 1989; Teotia *et al.*, 1992 and Sharma, 1999a).

Pathogen and disease cycle: The pathogen *Meloidogyne incognita* causes the disease. It has three stages in the life cycle *viz.* egg, larvae and adult. The eggs and larvae are the main sources of spread of the disease. A female lays 200-500 eggs in a gelatinous sac surrounding the posterior end of the female. Eggs are elongated, ovate whose bodies are about twice in length as broad as width. Eggs are 70-100 μ in length and 30-45 μ in width. They are white in colour initially, which turns brown at later stage. Larva is formed within the egg. It completes its first moult within the egg. The second stage larva is also pre-parasitic larva. It infect nearby cells within the gall where it is produced. The second stage larvae bore into the root and start feeding on the parenchymatous cells. Due to stimulus induced by the nematode, cells undergo repeated division and enlargement. As a result cancerous knots/galls appear on the root. The larvae undergo four moult and developed into mature female. Under favorable condition, eggs hatched into larvae and are liberated into the soil. The nematode takes 30-40 days to complete their life cycle in warm regions but in cold places, it may extend up to 67-69 days (Sengupta *et al.*, 1990). Nematode produces 6-7 generations within a year.

Pathogenic factors: Sandy soil with enough organic substances and sandy loam favors nematode infestation. Temperature from 15-35°C (optimum being 20-30°C), soil humidity of more than 60 per cent and soil pH of 4-8 are also favours development of nematodes (Murthy, 1986). As root knot nematodes are polyphagous and have a wide range of host plants, intercropping with any other host affects severely mulberry plants.

Economic Threshold Level

M. incognita causes significant reduction in mulberry plant growth and leaf yield at 1000 larvae/plant or more than

100 galls/plant or 150 larvae/250 cc soil under field conditions. Besides reducing the leaf production, it also affects the nutritive value by reducing the protein content, which is an important nutrient for silkworm growth. Feeding of the leaves harvested from infected plots affects growth of silkworms and quality of silk produced (Paul *et al.*, 1995). The magnitude of crop loss depends upon the population density of nematode present in the soil.

Control Measures

(i) Cultural control

- Cultural practices like repeated digging, weeding and exposure of soil to sunlight.
- Weeding out alternate host.
- Inter-cropping of Marigold (*Tagetus patula*), sesame (*Sesamum indicum*) or sun hemp (*Crotalaria spectabillis*) at 30 cm distance between mulberry rows reduces disease considerably. Mulching of these plants after full growth enriches the soil fertility in addition to controlling the disease (Govindaiah *et al.*, 1997).
- Avoiding planting of the nematode susceptible plants like maize, turmeric, tomato, etc. in and around the mulberry garden.
- Application of neem oil cake @ 2 MT/ha/yr in four equal split doses at an interval of 3 months is recommended for the control of this disease. Neem oil cake should thoroughly be incorporated in soil by digging or ploughing followed by irrigation (Sharma *et al.*, 1998). Adoption of this method also increases leaf yield due to increase in fertility of soil.
- Deep ploughing in the summer season, weeding etc., is also helpful; as physical control measure.

(ii) Chemical control

- Application of Organophosphate and Carbamate nematicides like Furadan 3G (Carbofuran) @ 40 kg/ha/yr in four equal split doses at an interval of 3 months along with fertilizer control the disease effectively. After application they should be well mixed in soil by digging/ploughing followed by irrigation. The leaf can be used for silkworm rearing after 40-50 days of nematicide application.

- Soil disinfections with Chloropicrin or Carbon disulphide or lime nitrogen is reported to be controlling the disease effectively (Ertian, 2003).

(iii) Biological control: Talc-based bionematicide (Bionema) produced by a bio-control agent, *Verticillium chlamydosporium* used along with neem oil cake reduces infestation (Sharma, 1999a). *Verticillium chlamydosporium* parasitises the eggs of *M. incognita* and stop further hatching, whereas the compounds present in the neem oil cake kill the nematode larvae present in the soil (Alam, 1993). The self-life of the product is 6 months under room temperature (25-30°C) and 10 months under low temperature (4-6°C).

For application mix 1 kg Bionema with 24 kg Neem oil cake and 200 kg FYM (sufficient for 1000 plants) and store the mixture with 25-30 per cent moisture for about one week under the shade. Expose the roots by digging at 15 cm deep and cut-off branches of knots from roots, wherever possible and destroy them. Apply the mixture @ 200 gm/plant around the exposed roots and broadcast the little amount in soil between plants. Apply the mixture 3 times in a year at an interval of 4 months during cultural operation/fertilizer application followed by irrigation. For one hectare per year, 80 kg Bionema, 20 MT-FYM and 2 MT neem oil cake are required. The technology is eco-friendly and effective. It reduces the disease severity by about 85-90 per cent and increase the leaf yield by 23 per cent. It is advised not to apply insecticide during application of bio-nematicide. The saplings having the knots should not be used for new plantation.

Cultivating nematode resistant mulberry varieties provides an alternative method in controlling nematode.

However, breeding of nematode resistant varieties has not received much attention and needs to be taken up on priority, since it would be more effective and highly economical method of nematode control. Relatively recently, mulberry varieties like S13, S30, S1096, RFS135 and V1 are reported moderately resistant to the disease. Root knot nematode incidence in mulberry is becoming severe in recent years. A multi-disciplinary approach for integrated crop management is the safest method for managing the disease cost-effectively and to boost cocoon production while protecting the environment from adverse effects of harmful pesticides.

(B) NON-INFECTIOUS/NON-PATHOGENIC/ PHYSIOLOGICAL DISEASES

Like other plants, mulberry often shows conspicuous symptoms of disorders/disease, even though no transmissible pathogen can be detected. Such symptoms are generally considered under the broad group—Non-parasitic Disorder (NPD).

The NPD's fall roughly into four categories:

(*a*) Deficiency and excess of minerals.

(*b*) Adverse meteorological conditions especially water deficit (due to drought and salinity).

(*c*) Pollutions.

(*d*) Genetic factors.

Once mulberry is planted, its foliage is generally utilized 4-6 times a year for 20 - 30 years from the same field, mostly through a continuous monoculture. As such, an enormous amount of nutrient replenishment is essential for a sustainable yield. On the other hand, a vast majority of mulberry garden (>70%) are maintained under rain-fed conditions at semi-arid or saline zones in India. Accordingly, research has focused, so far, on the disorders due to mineral deficiency and adverse meteorological conditions (especially on drought and salinity). This discussion is thus restricted and focused to these two topics only.

(*a*) Deficiency and Excess of Minerals

(*i*) **Mineral deficiency:** Approximately 16 elements are stated to be essential to the growth of most plants. Depending upon the quantity of requirements, essential elements are sub-divided into two groups –

Macronutrients: Those needed in relatively large quantities, usually e+ 1000 $\mu g/g^{-1}$ of dry matter. It includes Carbon (C), Hydrogen (H), Oxygen (O), Nitrogen (N), Phosphorus (P), Calcium (Ca), Sulphur (S), Potassium (K) and Magnesium (Mg) (total 9 elements).

Micronutrients: Those needed in considerably small amounts, usually d+ 100 $\mu g.g^{-1}$ of dry matter. It includes – Chlorine (Cl), Iron (Fe), Manganese (Mn), Boron (B) and Zinc (Zn), Copper (Cu) and Molybdenum (Mo) (total 7 elements). In mulberry, so far 11 elemental deficiency symptoms have been reported.

Causes of Mineral Deficiency

- Inadequate supply of one or more plant nutrients/ minerals in the soil or imbalance nutrient status.
- Element withdrawals due to continuous cultivation without proper replenishment.
- Imbalance in fertilizer application, especially nitrogen.
- Lack of proper use of microelements and organic nutrients.
- Changes in edaphic and/or abiotic factors such as soil pH, severe drought, alkalinity or salinity, loss of topsoil due to erosion (wind, water) etc.
- Increasing yield levels leads to higher nutrient requirement.
- Depletion of micronutrients due to intensive cultivation.
- Leaching out of micronutrients in the soil.
- Repeated or extreme use of one trace element may lead to imbalance of other elements.

Impact of Mineral Deficiency

- Primarily – quantitative and qualitative loss of foliage.
- Secondarily.
- Decrease in the intake of K, Ca, Mg and P causes decrease in body weight of the silkworm.
- P deficiency affects the uptake of other mineral elements affecting the growth and economic characters of silkworm.
- Deficiencies of Mg, Mn and Fe reduce the cocoon yield, shell weight and larval duration.
- Zn deficiency is known to decrease the pupal weight, silk filament length and cocoon shell ration.
- Besides, some non-essential (in respect of plants) elements such as Nickel (Ni) and Cobalt (Co) has a regulatory role on silk gland development.

(*ii*) Micronutrient Deficiency

Nitrogen (N): Nitrogen deficiency leads to reduced growth of mulberry (shoot, leaf and roots), reduced leaf area, prolonged bud dormancy, reduced shoot production and delayed flowering (Shankar, 1997).

Symptoms

- Arrest of terminal growth of plants besides slow and weak growth with less branching.
- Pale yellow leaves noticed first in older leaves.
- Yellowing proceeds from leaf tip to base.
- Leaf margin and base turn yellow with chlorosis on the advancement of age.
- In severe cases, young leaves become pale green and later turns yellow.
- Premature yellowing and dropping of leaves.
- Area nearer to veins is pronounced because of chlorosis.

- Root system also becomes stunted.
- Reduction in upper and lower epidermis and palisade layers.
- More spongy and total mesophyll layers.
- Starch grains are depleted, cell irregularly shaped and thin walled.
- Decrease in protein, nitrogen and chloroplast.
- Indicator—Nitrate reductase.

Management

- Maintaining soil pH between 6.5 and 7.5.
- Application of requisite quantity of nitrogen fertilizers (300-400 kg N/ha/yr in 4 to 5 split doses after 3-4 weeks of every harvest).
- Application of green leaf manure, FYM and tank silt @ 20-25 tonnes/ha/yr.
- Maintenance of soil moisture.
- Integrated nutrient management and foliar application of nitrogen.
- Regular application of nitrogen fixing bio-fertilizers along with FYM.

Phosphorus (P): Phosphorus deficiency results in reduced shoot height, leaf area and nutrient content of leaf (Radha *et al.*, 1988).

Symptoms

- Slender stem without fresh growth having stunted root system.
- Restricted root and shoot growth, suppressed shoot production, prolonged bud dormancy, decrease in number and size of flowers and early senescence of leaf (Shankar, 1997).

- Older leaves turn pale yellow; subsequently, the major veins and space between veins near the mid-rib regions of lamina will develop purplish and changes to brown colouration coupled with necrosis.
- Necrotic spots pronounced at margins. It increases from margin to the mid-rib region resulting in inward curling of leaves.
- Severely affected leaves show scorching in the margin, leaves becomes yellow and fall off prematurely.
- Reduction in thickness of upper and lower epidermis, mesophyll and palisade layer. Elongated cells with accumulation of starch grains in leaves (Shankar, 1997).
- Indicator – Acid phosphatase.

Management

- Apply 180 kg P_2O_5/ha/yr in equal split doses at alternate crops. It should be applied near to root zone at the depth of 20-40 cm from soil surface.

Deficiency of Phosphorus

Potassium (K): Potassium has been reported as a key nutrient in maintaining mulberry quality. Moisture content of leaf increases or decreases proportionately with potash contents of leaf (Radha *et al.*, 1988).

Symptoms

- Terminal growth ceases.
- The stem and root becomes slender.
- Older leaves show deficiency first.
- Yellow colouration and at times brown patches in margin of leaves.
- Necrotic spots extended towards base and mid-rib resulting in curling of leaves and leaves fall off prematurely.

Deficiency of Potassium

- Causing attack of powdery mildew disease, which is prominent on ventral surface of leaves.
- In advance stage, reduced leaf thickness.

- Shortening of internodes.
- Wilting of plants.
- Indicator – Arginine putrescine.

Management

- Maintenance of soil pH and soil moisture.
- Application of 180-240 kg K_2O/ha/yr based on soil test in two equal split doses after 3-4 weeks of 1st and 3rd harvest.
- Application of green manure, FYM and tank silt @ 20 - 25 tonnes/ha/yr.
- Integrated nutrient management and foliar application of potassium.

Calcium (Ca)

Symptoms

- Plant growth is completely ceased and becomes weak and lodged.
- The stem becomes woody and short with yellowing tips and the root becomes stubby and dry.
- Shape of leaf is distorted and younger leaves becomes more acute in shape *i.e.* deformation of younger leaves.
- Necrosis starts in margin and tip of the leaves.
- Older leaves are severely affected and show yellowing with mosaic green patches.
- Leaves starts falling in premature stage.
- Increased membrane leakage.

Management

- In acidic soil, apply lime one MT/ha/yr at the interval of every 4-5 years.
- Spray 0.5-1.0 per cent Calcium nitrate [$Ca(NO_3)_2$] or Calcium chloride ($CaCl_2$) over the leaves of deficient plant.

Magnesium (Mg)

Symptoms

- Plant growth is ceased.
- Chlorosis occurs in between the veins and is more prominent in younger leaves.
- Gradually chlorosis passes throughout the leaves.
- Leaves become totally yellow with reddish green patches all around the leaf.
- The leaf tips and margin become dried and scorched.
- Indicator—Pyruvate kinase.

Deficiency of Magnesium

Management

- Spray Magnesium sulphate of 0.2-0.5 per cent on deficient plants depending on the severity. If required, one more dose can be sprayed after 5-7 days of first spray.

Iron (Fe)

Symptoms

- Overall plant growth is not very much affected.
- Pronounced interveinal chlorosis and reticulate appearance.
- Younger leaves are almost green but with chlorotic patches.
- Lower leaves become golden yellow in colour having dusty look.
- Chloroplast size reduced.
- Indicator-Polyphenol oxidase, peroxidase, catalase.

Management

- Aqueous solution of one kg Ferrous sulphate/ha/crop should be sprayed over the leaves of deficient plants.
- Fe Chelates like EDDHA @ 100 kg/ha should be mixed in soil in iron deficient fields.

Zinc (Zn)

Symptoms

- Overall plant growth is arrested.
- Lower leaves become yellowish green.
- Severe reduction in leaf size.
- Whitish spots appear on the older leaves.
- Decrease in auxin content.
- Interveinal chlorosis *i.e.* chlorosis is more pronounced towards vein.
- Indicator—Carbonic anhydrase.

Management

- Aqueous solution of 2 kg Zinc sulphate/ha/crop should be sprayed over the leaves of deficient mulberry plants.

Copper (Cu)

Symptoms

- Plant growth is ceased.
- Leaves fall in premature stage.
- Younger leaves are yellow and wilting starts from the tip of the leaf.
- Chlorosis starts from the margin of the leaf.
- Yellowish spots are observed throughout the leaf.
- Basic amino acid levels unusually high.
- Indicator—Ascorbic acid oxidase.

Deficiency of Copper

Management

- Aqueous solution of one kg Copper sulphate/ha/crop should be sprayed over deficient plants.

Boron (B)

Symptoms

- Plant growth is slowed down and young tissues disintegrate.

- Stem and veins of the leaves proliferate and protrude out.
- Cambial tissue degenerate causes the plants to crack, blacken or become abnormal in shape.

Management

- Spray aqueous solution of one kg Boric acid (Borax)/ha/crop over the leaves of deficient plants.

Manganese (Mn)

Symptoms

- Ceased plant growth.
- Chlorosis starts from the margin in younger leaves and spreads towards whole leaf.
- In mature leaves, chlorosis is found towards veins and yellowish white spots are found throughout the leaf.

Management

- Spray aqueous solution of one kg Manganese sulphate/ha/crop over the deficient plants.

Sulphur (S): Sulphur is one of the sixteen nutrient elements, essential for the growth and development of mulberry. It is involved in the formation of chlorophyll and glucosides and in the activation of enzymes. It improves mulberry leaf yield and nutritional quality. In case of deficiency of sulphur, the full potential of a crop can not be realized regardless of application of other nutrients. The causes of deficiency of sulphur includes increasing depletion of soil sulphur through higher yields, wide gap between the removal and addition of sulphur, inadequate recycling of crop residues, loss of sulphur through leaching and soil erosion besides low level of fertilizer sulphur input.

Symptoms

- The stem becomes slender.
- Overall growth of the plant is stunted with general lack of new growth.
- Necrosis starts from the margin in younger leaves. Brownish oily spots are observed throughout on the leaves.
- Lower leaves become yellow and fall in pre-mature stage.

Management

- 0.1-0.2 per cent aqueous solution of Potassium sulphate should be sprayed on deficient plants.

Deficiency of Sulphur

(iii) Excess of minerals: Disorders due to excess of minerals are very uncommon in mulberry, mainly because cultivable genotypes of mulberry are high input responsive and their "luxurious consumption level" is expected to be high.

However, some of the sporadic disorders due to excess application of nitrogenous fertilizer are –

- Leaves are unusually dark green.
- Abundance of foliage but poorly developed root system.
- Leaf area increased enormously but thickness is reduced.

Nutrient Deficiency—Factors

There are several factors, which can inhibit proper nutrition of mulberry plant leading to nutrient deficiency *viz.*, pH, inadequate supply of chemical fertilizer, water stress, low soluble salts, mineral antagonism, temperature, diseases etc.

pH: The soil pH is an important factor that can cause nutrient deficiency in mulberry plants. The ideal pH for luxuriant growth of mulberry plants is 6.2 to 6.8. If soil pH value is higher, there will be poor uptake of boron, copper, iron, manganese and zinc and if soil pH is lower than the recommended, there will be less availability of nutrients like calcium and magnesium.

Inadequate supply of chemical fertilizer: Supply of inadequate quantity of chemical fertilizer can cause deficiency of nutrients in soil. The soil may not have sufficient levels of nutrient to meet plant growth requirement or environmental conditions sometimes may prevent the nutrient from being accessible to the plants. Plants not receiving balanced nutrition are often more susceptible to attack by insect and disease causing organisms and damage by extreme environmental conditions.

Water stress: Constant flood irrigation of land can cause micro and macro-nutrient deficiency. As over watering inhibit oxygen levels affecting water uptake by root system. Also inactivity of root systems due to saturated conditions can lead to inefficient uptake of iron or phosphorus leading to chlorosis.

Low soluble salts: Soluble salts are total dissolved salts in the soil at any given time and are measured in terms of Electrical Conductivity (EC). When the EC content of soil is too low, plant growth gets stunted and mineral deficiency occur. Deficiency in mulberry plants such as lower leaf yellowing (nitrogen), lower leaf purpling (phosphorus) and lower leaf inter-venial chlorosis (magnesium) are common when water values are lower.

Mineral antagonism: When certain elements are provided in excess to plants, uptake of other nutrients may get hindered is known as mineral antagonism. It has been established that any one of the potassium-calcium-magnesium elements in excess can cause decrease in the uptake of the other. Excess phosphorus can cause a decrease in uptake of zinc, iron and copper.

Temperature: Temperature also plays a significant role in the introduction of nutrient deficiency in mulberry. Temperature below 55^0F affects phosphorus uptake. Purpling of the lower foliage is the common symptom.

Disease: Plant pathogens, such as *Fusarium* and *Pythium* feed on the nutrients in roots causing inefficient uptake of minerals by plants.

(*b*) Adverse Environmental Conditions

(i) Water deficit stress: Water deficit elicits a complex of plant responses beginning with stress perception, which initiates a signal transduction pathway(s) and manifested in changes in cellular, physiological and developmental levels. The responses depend on:

- Severity and duration of stress.
- Plant genotype and developmental stage.

In agriculture, average or poor yield and lower harvest index of economically important plants, are the main characteristics, even in water stress tolerant genotypes. Cellular water deficit may result from stress like—high and low temperature, drought/desiccation and salt (mainly salinity). The later two are most important in tropical mulberry.

(ii) Drought stress: Drought may be defined as absence of adequate rainfall or irrigation for a period of time long enough to result in depletion of soil water and injury to plant. While, drought resistance includes, a range of mechanism(s) by which plant overcome the stress.

Inevitable Sericulture in Drought Prone Areas

- Recurring drought has been recognized as a single most important limitation of agricultural productivity in almost every part of India.
- 80 per cent of mulberry cultivable areas are at semi-arid tropics in India.
- Mulberry is still cultivated as a rain-fed crop in < 70 per cent of areas in India and faces intermittent to moderate drought.

Research Strategies Adopted to Cope with Drought

Dehydration tolerance has been investigated using three main approaches in plants:

- Examining already tolerant system, such as seed, xerophytes.
- Analysing mutants from genetic models of biochemically better explored plants, such as *Aradiopsis thaliana, L. esculentum* and *Nicotiana* spp.
- Analysing the effects of stress on existing genotypes of agriculturally important crops (mesophytes) and selection of tolerant genotypes under moderate limits of stress. Mulberry belongs to this group.

What Happens during Drought in Mesophytes?

(Mild to moderate stress model when system is elastic)

- Signal perception in root.
- Root measures soil dryness by mechanical impedance by a change in soil strength (Ψ-0.1 to -0.2 MPa).
- Root sourced (not leaf sourced)—ABA may transduce drought signal to shoot.
- Cell enlargement (in younger leaf) is first arrested due to low water uptake
- (Ψ-0.1 to -0.3 MPa).
- Narrowing of stomata and slow gas exchange.
- Leaf start to act as photosynthetic sink, photo assimilates are partly used as osmotic adjustment and partly partitioned to root.
- General loss of protein synthesis but drought induced protein levels increase enormously.
- Increase root—shoot ratio and limited leaf area expansion, allow avoidance of development of larger root to leaf gradient potential.
- Osmotic adjustment protects the cell(s) from extreme desiccation and allows a continued minimal gas exchange (Ψ-0.3 to -0.6 MPa).
- Cytokinines decrease in leaves and cell division reduced ((Ψ-0.4 to -0.8 MPa).
- Older leaf senesce and thus leaf area decreases.
- Amino acid—proline, some sugars and sugar alcohol level increased (Ψ-0.6 to -1.0 MPa).

As bulk of leaf tugger is maintained in living cells by osmotic adjustment, partially fixed carbon is utilized for minimal architecture maintenance. The plant usually recovers if watered in this stage (Ψ-0.8 to -2.0 MPa) and tolerant cultivars are less affected.

Strategies of drought screening in mulberry: So far, drought-screening studies have been conducted in the following directions—

(i) Parameters Associated with Dehydration Postponement

(a) *Morphological:* Rooting potential, root volume and mass, root growth rate, leaf area, internodal distance, canopy architecture, leaf temperature, leaf and cuticular thickness, root: shoot ratio etc.

(b) *Anatomical:* Stomatal frequency, size, palisade to spongy parenchyma ratio, cuticular wax etc.

(ii) Parameter Associated with Dehydration Resistance

- In situ leaf gas exchange parameters like net photosynthesis rate, transpiration rate, stomatal resistance, diffusive resistance and physiological water use efficiency.
- Water status—RWC, water deficit per cent, leaf keeping quality.
- Osmolytes titre—proline and other amino acids, sucrose and Na^+, K^+, Ca^{2+}.
- Indicators—ABA, glutathione reductase, nitrate reductase.

Bio-assay: Bioassay of short listed genotypes with suitable silkworm breeds.

Trials: Field yield trails and recommendation.

Saline Stress

Salinity is an environmental stress that limits growth and development in plants. The response of plants to excess NaCl is complex and involves changes in their morphology, physiology and metabolism. In mulberry, most study has been descriptive and has not elucidated mechanisms by which salinity inhibits plant growth. There are multiple genes that seem to act in concert to increase NaCl tolerance and certain proteins involved in salinity stress protection have been recognized, in other plants.

Table 3.4: Recommended Mulberry Genotypes for Drought Prone Areas

Genotype	Characters	Leaf yield	Recommended for
S_{13}	Fast growing, high rootability and moisture retention capacity, high leaf moisture content (>76%), short internodes	18 MT/ha/yr	Red soil zone of South India specially Karnataka and Tamil Nadu
S_{34}	Deep and extensive root system, high moisture retention capacity, large leaf size.	17 MT/ha/yr	Black soil of South India specially Karnataka
C_{1730}	High rootability, high photosynthetic potential and physiological water use efficiency, high Osmolite levels, ABA and glutathione reductase activity.	13 MT/ha/yr	Red laterite soil of Bankura and Purulia districts of West Bengal

Sericulture in Saline Soil

- In India >7 million hectares of land is salt affected and at present it has become a pervasive problem in newly irrigated arid and semi-arid tropics as well as coastal belts under cultivation.
- Mulberry is a fast growing cash crop and is widely advocated for cultivation, not only for sericulture, but also for wasteland management in rain-fed areas.

Sericulture Zones Affected by Salinity

- Coastal districts of Tamil Nadu and Andhra Pradesh, 24 Parganas (S) and southern part of Midnapore of West Bengal.
- A total of 15-20 per cent of mulberry cultivable land is affected by moderate to high degree of salinity.
- In West Bengal the total estimated saline area is 0.82 million hectare and the entire area is monocropped with rice.

Critical Injury Level and Symptom(s) of Salinization

- For mulberry, ca. 6.0 $ds.cm^{-1}$ Electrical Conductivity (EC) of soil (due to NaCl) is highly toxic for rooting and sprouting of all tested genotypes.
- Moderate to high degree of desiccation due to the failure of transpiration stream in some genotypes.
- However, other morphological symptoms are inconsistent, almost all-important symptoms are at the cellular level.

What Happens during Saline Stress?

Mulberry is basically subjected to three types of adverse condition during NaCl stress:

(*a*) Water deficit due to osmoticum

(*b*) Mineral toxicity due to salt accumulation

(*c*) Disturbance in mineral nutrition due to imbalance of essential mineral availability at target tissue.

The first site of salinity perception is the root. Abscisic acid (ABA) and cytokinin (CK) are most likely mediators of signals from root to shoot. The soil may accumulate high salt level, even water potential of 24 bars and above. As the water (containing solutes) moves from negative to more negative water potential, in a soil-plant-air continuum, by adjusting/developing a large soil to air gradient, unable to meet the transpiration demands, they wilt and desiccate. Before that, plants adjust osmotically and may not show symptoms of wilting up to a certain limit. Different morphometric parameters indirectly, and various cellular components directly have been associated with these osmotic adjustment and regulation of accumulated salts.

Strategies to Overcome Saline Stress in Mulberry

- The soil reclamation and drainage practices are generally applied in orchard and green house crops, which proved ineffective and costly approach for mulberry.
- Molecular biological approaches to over or under expression of some targeted genes related with osmotic adjustment are yet to get proper impetus in mulberry due to:
  - The genetics of these highly heterogenous species is poorly understood.
  - Basic physio biochemical pathways in mulberry are less explored.
- Selection of salinity tolerant genotypes by evaluating morphometric and physio biochemical indices and correlation of such parameters with leaf yield and silkworm bioassay has been adopted so far.

Parameters for the Selection of Saline Stress Tolerant Genotypes

(i) Morphometric: Rooting potential, average root length, root and leaf biomass, total leaf area, epicuticular wax etc.

(ii) Element Titre: Na, K, Ca and Cl in leaves and roots, K: Na ratio.

(iii) Osmolytes: Proline and quaternary ammonium compounds, sugar(s) (sucrose, cellulose) and sugar alcohols (sorbitol and inositol).

(iv) Silkworm feeding stimulant: Iso-quercitrin, morin and sitosterol.

(v) Water status: RWC, WDP, Moisture retention capacity.

(vi) Silkworm bioassay

(vii) Field yield trial.

Table 3.5 : Saline Tolerant Genotypes of Mulberry

Geno-type	Characters	Leaf yield	Recommen-ded for
BC-259	High rooting potential, high N and K ratio, moderate Na, K, Ca level, high Osmolite level, higher VAM infectivity and photosynthetic potential	18 MT/ha/yr	Coastal areas to Tamil Nadu, Andhra Pradesh.
C_{776}	High root ability, high leaf yields potential and better silkworm bioassay performance.	25 MT/ha/yr (with irrigation)	Saline prone areas of West Bengal *viz.* 24 Parganas (S), Howrah, Midnapore.

INTEGRATED DISEASE MANAGEMENT (IDM)

Following the introduction of Integrated Pest Management (IPM) practice in the field of pest control, pathologists all over the world also showed same interest for development of integrated disease management practice. It is suggested that, for satisfactory control of most plant diseases it requires integration of several procedures including manipulation of microenvironment. In the field of mulberry crop protection, progress in the fundamental areas of research appropriate to IDM is considerable. The research findings of mulberry diseases show the integrated management in mulberry protection is possible by the integration of following disease management practices.

(*i*) Cultural Control

(a) Site Selection: Soil type climate and altitude, may control health and vigour of mulberry plant. Moreover, the physical characteristics of the soil such as temperature, moisture content and texture have an impact on occurrence and survival of pathogenic micro-organisms in the soil, for example, volcanic ash soil favours development of violet root rot (*Helicobasidium mompa*) suggesting root rot resistant varieties for this region. Varietal resistance sometimes depends on the environment where the plant grows. Variety, MR2 is found resistant to powdery mildew in hills while in plains its resistance power is low.

(b) Planting density: Severity of many diseases is found higher in closer spacing (30×60 cm) compared to wider spacing.

(c) Digging and sun drying: Digging loosens the soil for better aeration and nitrification. It also plays an important role in controlling many diseases of mulberry. Repeated digging of the fields before or after plantation especially just after pruning of mulberry, facilitate soil solarisation, which may help to eradicate many diseases by increasing the soil temperature. It is observed that intensity of dwarf disease is mild at high light intensity and severe at low light intensity. Pathogen like *Fusarium lateratium* and *F. solani* are abundant in soil from spring to summer than from autumn to winter, indicating that rising of soil temperature is not in favour of pathogen. Also adoption of digging and clipping of side roots favours nematode disease control. It is suggested to adopt deep digging in summer to kill nematode eggs and larvae by strong sunlight and high soil temperature.

(d) Sanitation and farm hygiene: Eradication of harmful weed hosts, the timely destruction of fallen diseased leaves and twigs will reduce the disease intensity. Many pathogens over-winter through their resting spores or fruiting bodies on the dead plants. Many pathogens including nematodes are having weeds as secondary hosts. Removing the weeds in the field can solve this problem.

(e) Pruning: Pruning is an important practice solely to improve the yield of mulberry foliage. It also improves the feeding value of leaves by minimizing the disease severity. Pruning of the infected branches during the early bacterial blight development is reported to minimize the disease severity. It is also suggested to control powdery mildew by cutting off the branches followed by spraying of suitable fungicide.

(f) Irrigation, mulching, manuring and fertilization: These practices in general, promote rapid growth and shorten the susceptible stage of the plant. At the same time, manuring and fertilization makes it easier for the plant to overcome both infectious and non-infectious diseases. In spite of these, the dosage of manure and fertilizer which has been determined depending upon the system of planting, age of the plant, spacing and soil type control several physiological disorders such as chlorosis and weak growth by nitrogen, marginal scorching by potassium intra venial chlorosis by phosphorus, necrosis and defoliation of young leaves by calcium, chlorosis and necrotic spots on leaves by magnesium and chlorosis and lack of growth by sulphur. Irrigation alone has no positive effect on mulberry disease control. It increases bacterial leaf blight, *Cercospora* and *Pseudocercospora* leaf spot. Powdery mildew incidence in the irrigated field is reported to be lower than that of non-irrigated. This may be due to the destruction of cleistothecia by water logging. Regarding mulching, it is reported that, mulching with green leaves of Pongamia and neem in soil decreases both the number of nematodes and their egg mass. The nematicidal activity of marigold is also observed. Thus the growing of marigold in the nematode infested field and mulching after a certain period of growth may also be a very effective control measure for the disease.

(*ii*) Biological Control

The role of naturally occurring enemies has been studied for a number of pathogens and pests, and in many cases, they have been found to play a significant role in reducing disease incidence. In mulberry, phylloplane micro-organisms such as *Cladosporium cladosporoides, Curvularia lunata, Pseudomonas maltophylla* are found strong antagonistic to *Cercospora moricola* in *in-vitro* and in *in-vivo* condition. *Cladosporium cladosporoides* also reported to parasitise on *Phyllactinia corylea.*

Some Coccinellid insects play a significant role in mulberry disease control. Grubs and adults of ladybird beetle, *Illeus indica* and *Illeus cincta,* found to eat the conidia and hyphal mass of Phyllactinia corylea. In addition release of 8-10 predacious beetle of *Cryptolaemus montrouzieri* during early infestation of tukra has been suggested as an effective control measure.

(*iii*) Resistant Varieties

Prevention is better than cure. Planting of resistant mulberry varieties is to be given priority as a disease control measure. Many of the mulberry varieties are reported to be resistant to diseases. Variety, Kenmochi is resistant to twig blight; Buriram-60 to powdery mildew; S54, S36, S799, OPH-1, AB x Phill and MR2 to leaf spot and powdery mildew; Ukrane-510 to brown leaf spot; Husang, Schinichinose, Hyatesakari and Manamisakari to leaf blight. Also, C763 and S1 are reported resistant to tukra.

(*iv*) Chemical Control

(a) Treatment of soil: Soil fumigation by chloropicrin @ 450 g/m^2 is suggested to control both violet and red root rot. The soil fungicide, Parachloronitrobenzene (PCNB) is found suitable for root rot and other soil borne diseases. Wilt disease of sprouted mulberry cuttings infected by *Sclerotium rolfsii* can be controlled by drenching 0.2 per cent solution of PCNB. Application of Aldecarp or Carbo furan @ 30 kg/ ha/yr in 4 equal split doses to get effective control of nematode disease. It was observed that, the cleistothecia of *P. corylea* over wintering on dormant mulberry shoots in the field were completely eradicated with single application of PCNB or Pentachlorophenol.

(b) Fungicide sprays: Several fungicides are recommended for the foliar diseases. Bavistin 0.1 per cent is recommended for the control of powdery mildew as well as leaf spot disease caused by *Cercospora moricola, Pseudocercospora and Myrothecium roridum.* Indofil 0.2 per cent gave better result for the control of leaf spot diseases. Sulfex 0.2 per cent is reported to control powdery mildew and also Blitox and Kavach are reported against leaf rust disease.

Further, forewarning system are to be developed for the diseases indicating relation between meteorological parameters and the disease appearance to develop an effective management system in order to decide the time of application of different fungicides, pruning and other control measures for prevention and control of diseases.

Control of Mulberry Diseases through Plant Extracts and Bio-control Agents

Mulberry (*Morus* sp.) is affected by several diseases like powdery mildew, leaf spot, leaf rust, bacterial leaf spot, root knot etc. Though a few fungicide/antibiotics like, Bavistin, Sulfex, Blitox, Pushamycin etc. have already been recommended, but several factors determine the use of such synthetic chemicals.

- High cost.
- Residual toxicity to silkworm.
- Indiscriminate use results in evolution of resistant strain of pathogen.

- Continuous uses of chemical pesticides also pollute environment.
- Eliminate useful flora and fauna.
- Harmful to human and other animals in long run.

Of late scientists are searching for eco-friendly management of diseases through plant based pesticides and bio-control agents.

Plant Extracts

The different plant extracts have been used to plant disease control due to their proven nature of specificity, easy biodegradability and eco-friendly nature. In mulberry, several workers have established efficacy of plant extracts for control of important diseases, like Powdery mildew, *Cercospora* leaf spot, *Myrothecium* leaf spot, Bacterial leaf spot and Root knot.

Table 3.6 : Disease Control by Plant Extracts

Disease	Effective plant extracts
Powdery mildew	*Azadirachta indica, Chromoleana odorata, Adhatoda zeylanica*
Cercospora leaf spot	*Eucalyptus sp.* and *Calotrpis gigentia*
Myrothecium leaf spot	*Eucalyptus sp* and *Allium sp.*
Bacterial leaf spot	*Eucalyptus sp*
Root knot	*Acaciacides* (A plant based systemic nematocides)

Biological Control

In recent years biological control received much attention due to reorganization of problem associated with the use of pesticides. Biological control is defined as the activities of any biological organism that function as a control mechanism for any economically significant pest or plant disease-causing organism. In biological control, micro-organisms operate through:

(*a*) Antibiosis

(*b*) Competition

(*c*) Parasitism

(*d*) Induced systemic resistance.

In mulberry several soil borne diseases are successfully control through bio-control agents.

Table 3.7 : Mulberry Soil Borne Diseases Controlled by Bio-control Agents

Disease	Bio-control Agents
Stem canker, Cutting rot, Collar rot	**Nursery Guard** (a bio formulation of *Trichoderma pseudokoningii*)
Root rot	**Raksha** (a bio-formulation of *Trichoderma harzianum*)
Root Knot	**Bionema** (*Verticillium chlamydosporium* and neem oil cake)

Decomposed Extract

Since early 1970, compost extracts utilized effectively for control of plant disease caused by soil born pathogen. In mulberry decomposed extracts of *Catharanthus roseus, Murrya koningii* and *Eupotarium odarata* control powdery mildew disease at par with chemical fungicides.

Assessment of Crop Loss in Mulberry

Various diseases of mulberry cause huge crop loss if they are not controlled in proper time. This loss can be termed as qualitative and quantitative loss. Both of this ultimately causes economic loss to farmers from the crop. Accurate estimation of crop loss due to different diseases is cumbersome, since the loss depends on various factors such as mulberry variety, age of the mulberry plantation, season, disease intensity and many other factors. The extent and type of damage may vary from disease to disease depending on the host plants response to the particular pathogen or host pathogen interaction. Some pathogens may cause complete devastation of mulberry plantation while some cause very little damage to the crop and hence the overall crop loss due to different diseases is yet to be estimated. However, various studies were conducted to assess the crop loss due to some important diseases such as leaf spot and powdery mildew. It is estimated about 9.9 per cent to 11.5 per cent leaf yield loss due to *Cercospora* leaf spot and 5.5 to 10.3 per cent due to powdery mildew. In sericulture, since leaf is not the end product, the actual loss due to disease will only be reflect in the end product and hence, the assessment of end product loss due to diseases and ultimate monetary loss or economic loss are to be considered. Some attempts are made in the recent past to assess the cocoon loss and resulting monetary loss due to feeding powdery mildew and leaf spot infected mulberry leaves at different intensity levels. It was estimated that, if the mulberry suffer from >50 per cent disease severity due to leaf spot, (*Cercospora moricola / Myrothecium roridum*), the maximum product loss of 54.58 and monetary loss of 61.28 while due to powdery mildew it was, 55.58 and 64.44. The loss can be termed as qualitative loss and quantitative loss.

Leaf Yield Loss

The quantitative loss or yield loss generally cause due to the necrosis of the leaves, defoliation, reduction in leaf production and the mortality of mulberry plants. The quantitative loss due to diseases can be assessed comparing the yield from protected mulberry plot and the non-protected mulberry plot as follows:

$$\text{Leaf yield loss (\%)} = \frac{\text{Leaf yield in protected plot-leaf yield in unprotected}}{\text{Leaf yield in protected plot}} \times 100$$

For protection of a plot from a particular disease, the plants are to be treated with suitable effective and recommended solution.

Qualitative loss is very important aspect since the quality of the mulberry leaf fed to the silkworms is the important determinant of the quality of silk. This includes loss in nutritive contents of the leaves. Since the disease cause physiological process such as photosynthesis, this qualitative loss generally cause due to the physiological alteration in the host system after pathogen invasion. The physiological activities generally affect due to the pathogen invasion are, photosynthesis, transpiration, stomatal conductance, moisture content and water translocation. Alteration in these activities cause the alteration in the biochemical processes in the plant system and ultimately leads to the reduction in the biochemical constituents. Biochemical analysis of leaf spot and powdery mildew infected leaves showed reduction in protein, sugar, starch, other carbohydrates and minerals. This leads to the reduction in the nutritive value of leaves. Feeding powdery mildew infected leaves to silkworms showed prolonged larval duration and weak worms in the mature stage.

Cocoon Crop Loss

Cocoon is the ultimate product due to silkworm rearing. Nutritive value of the leaves fed will reflect in the cocoons obtained after rearing. The cocoon yield loss can be assessed by comparing the cocoon yield obtained after rearing with leaves from diseased mulberry plot and cocoon yield obtained after rearing with leaves from the protected plot.

In terms of quantity, the characters such as Effective Rearing Rate (ERR) by weight and number, weight of mature larvae, single cocoon weight and single shell weight are adversely influenced by rearing silkworms with powdery mildew and leaf spot infected mulberry leaves.

Important qualitative and commercial characters such as SR per cent, silk recovery, filament length are also found reduced due to feeding powdery mildew and leaf spot infected mulberry leaves. Due to reduction of quality of cocoon and the silk content, the farmers only get a low income from such poor quality end product. Also, it was observed that, grainage parameters such as fecundity, hatching percentage are adversely influenced due to feeding silkworm with disease-infected leaves.

Estimation of Quantity of Fungicide Required

The quantity of fungicide required to spray can be calculated using the following formula:

$$P = \frac{V \times C}{F}$$

Where P = Quantity of fungicide required;

V = Volume of solution to be prepared;

C = Concentration of solution desired;

F = Concentration of commercial formulation.

Forecasting of Pests and Diseases

(I) PEST SURVEILLANCE AND FORECASTING

(A) Pest Surveillance

Pest surveillance is defined as 'periodical assessment of pests populations and their damage' or 'watch kept on a pest for the purpose of decision-making in pest management'. Pest surveillance can provide the necessary information to determine the feasibility of a pest control programme. Method of sampling, surveillance and forecasting of insect population for integrated pest management in sericulture is described by Singh *et al.*, 2004. Pest surveillance comprises of three basic components:

- Determination of the level of incidence of pest species
- Determination of what loss the incidence will cause
- Determination of economic benefits the control will provide.

(i) Objectives of pest surveillance

- To monitor the presence of a pest
- To determine the population density, dispersion, damage caused etc.

(ii) Survey: Regular survey activity is necessary for successful surveillance programmes. An insect pest survey is 'a detailed collection of insect population information at a particular time in a given area'. These surveys are both qualitative and quantitative. The qualitative surveys aim at the pest detection, employed with newly introduced pests and often precedes quantitative survey. The quantitative surveys attempt to define numerically the abundance of an insect population in time and space. It is useful to predict future population trends and to assess damage potentials.

(iii) Sampling: It is 'a representative part of the total population and base our estimate on that part'.

(iv) Sampling techniques: Surveillance requires suitable sampling techniques. A sampling technique is 'the method used to collect information for a single sample'. The sampling techniques include direct counts (in-situ counts); knock down, netting, trapping (use of light trap, pheromone trap and sticky trap), extraction from soil etc.

(v) Sampling programme: It is 'the procedure for employing the sampling techniques in time and space'. Sampling programme describes when sampling is to begin, location of samples, number of samples and how often samples should be taken.

(vi) Scientific surveillance methodologies: A scientific surveillance methodology consists of fixed plot surveys, roving surveys and monitoring through light pheromone and sticky traps.

(a) *Fixed plot survey:* In an acre plot, five micro plots of m^2 area are marked one each in four corners (1 m away from bund) and fifth in the centre of the chosen field. Periodical assessment is done in these micro plots. These plots are to be kept free from chemical sprays till the ETL is reached.

(b) *Roving survey:* This is conducted every week in randomly selected field plots along the prescribed route of the survey. Observations are recorded from the west corner by a diagonal walk to 100 m.

(vii) Decision-making: Decision-making is the keystone in insect pest management programmes. It indicates the course of action to be taken in any pest situation. Identification of pest, biology and behaviour of the pests, natural regulating factors, need for control measures, timing of control measures and selection of suitable control measures are critical factors in decision-making.

(viii) Indices in pest surveillance

(a) *Economic damage:* It is 'the amount of injury, which justifies the cost of artificial control measures'.

(b) *Economic injury level (EIL):* It is defined, 'as the lowest number of insects that will cause economic damage' 'or' the 'cost of control measures equal to yield loss by insects'.

(c) *Economic thresh-hold level (ETL):* It is 'the level at which management action should be taken to prevent population reaching EIL'.

Factors Affecting the ETL

- Crop value/market value;
- Management costs;
- Degree of injury;
- Crop susceptibility to injury.

The relationship between ETL and market value is inverse. The crop market value is always under fluctuations. Management costs tend to be more stable than crop market value. The degree of injury by various type of feeding is also important. The relationship between injury and the crop yield is the most important factor of the ETL.

$$\text{Gain thresh-hold} = \frac{\text{Management cost (Rs./acre)}}{\text{Market value (Rs./kg)/acre}} = \text{kg/ac}$$

$$\text{EIL} = \frac{\text{Gain thresh-hold}}{\text{Loss per insect}}$$

(B) Forecasting

It is 'an advance knowledge of probable pest infestations (out breaks) in a crop for planning the cropping pattern in such a way as to minimize the damage but also to get the best advantage of the pest control measures' or 'forewarning of the forthcoming infestations of pests'.

Forecasts are being done based on populations studies, studies on the pest's life history and field studies of the effect of climatic factors on the pest and its environment. Forecasting service serves (*i*) to predict the forthcoming infestation level of the pest, which is essential in justifying the use of control measures and (*ii*) to find out the critical stage at which the applications of insecticides would afford maximum protection. The forecasts may be of two types *viz.*

(i) Short-term forecasting: It covers a particular season or two successive seasons and it is based on simple sampling.

(ii) Long-term forecasting: It covers large areas and it is based on possible effects of weather on the insect abundance or by extrapolating from the present population density into the future.

The distribution of pests and the extent of damage caused by them are directly related to the frequency of incidence. Hence, forecasting extent of incidence, damage and range of pest population has to be taken into account. In fact, this type of forecast raises two standards *i.e.* standard for quantum of incidence and standard for forecasting incidence durations. Shorter the forecasting period higher is the accuracy. Contrarily, with increase in other influential factors, accuracy suffers. Currently, systematic scientific data are lacking for assessment (forecast) reports on mulberry pests. Also the forecasts for the time of pest incidence are not as perfect as those of food grains, cotton and other crops. There is an urgent need for proper data accumulation to improve the accuracy of assessment of impact of pest in mulberry plantation. The principle aim of pest forecasting is to ensure that control measures, notably the use of chemical pesticides, are adopted only when needed to prevent economic damage and at the correct time for maximum effectiveness. This would help to ensure that chemicals are used to supplement 'natural controls', as well as minimizing the problems created by overuse and misuse of pesticides. Forecasting is therefore, fundamental to many Integrated Pest Management (IPM) programmes. Three major components are involved in developing and implementing the forecasting scheme:

- Defining the economic threshold for pest attack;
- Developing relevant monitoring and forecasting procedures;
- Providing a means for implementing the forecasting programme within the crop production system.

The first consideration is to assess whether a practical forecast is feasible, given the nature of the particular pest problem, the objectives of the grower and the control options available. Much will depend upon whether early levels of pest incidence can be related to future levels of damage on the crop.

(iii) Safe period: Since silkworms are highly sensitive to pesticides, harvest of mulberry leaves before the safe period should be avoided. In case, if this is not followed strictly and contaminated leaves are harvested from the garden either located adjacent to field crops applied with pesticides or directly treated with pesticide, silkworm larvae develop toxic symptoms (vomiting of the digestive juice, swinging of the anterior half of the body, shortening of the body due to loss of the body fluid, paralysis etc) followed by the loss of the crop. Based on the studies conducted, calendar of events and 'ready reckoner' for chemical control measures of important mulberry pests have been developed which is briefly summarized on next pages (Table 4.1 and 4.2).

Table 4.1: Ready Reckoner for Chemical Control (Govindaiah *et al.*, 2005)

S.N	Name of the pest	Insecticide (EC %)	Required concentration (%)	Quantity per litre water	Safe period (days)
1.	Mealy bug	DDVP 76%	0.20	2.63 ml	17
2.	Leaf roller	DDVP 76%	0.076	1 ml	7
3.	Bihar hairy caterpillar	DDVP 76%	0.15	2 ml	9
4.	Jassids	DDVP 76%, Dimethoate 30%	0.076, 0.10	1 ml 3.3 ml	8 6
5.	Thrips	Dimethoate 30%	0.20	6.6 ml	10
6.	Scale insects	DDVP 76%	0.15	2 ml	9
7.	Grasshopper	DDVP 76%	0.15	2 ml	9
8.	Stem girdler	DDVP 76%	0.20	2.6 ml per injection	17
9.	Termites	Chloropyriphos 20%	0.08	2 ml	12

(iv) Volume of pesticide required per unit area: In a pesticide application programme, it is very essential to know the volume of spraying or dusting material required for an effective coverage of an area. If the volume of liquid to be sprayed is taken more, the pesticide will be wasted and the effective concentration will be less. On the other hand, if the volume of the liquid taken is less, it may not cover the entire field and the effective concentration may be more. In mulberry with 2′×2′ spacing the volume of the solution required has been estimated as 200 litre/acre.

(v) Calculation for dilution: Commercial formulations of pesticides are generally marketed in concentrated forms, while for pest control; very low percentages of the active

Table 4.2 : Safe Periods of other Commonly used Pesticides

Name of insecticides*	Concentration (% active ingredients)	Safe period (in days)
Demeton (Metasystox)	0.01 0.05	11 13
Aldrin (Aldrex)	0.01 0.05	11 13
Phosphomidon (Dimecron)	0.01 0.05	11 13
DDVP (Dichlorovos, Nuvan)	0.01 0.05	07 11
Methlyparathion (Metacid)	0.01 0.05	07 13
Carbaryl (Sevimol)	0.05 0.10	09 11
Quinalphos (Ekalux)	0.05 0.10	07 13
Dimethoate (Rogor)	0.05 0.10	07 11
Endosulfan (Thiodan)	0.05 0.10	09 17
Phosalone (Zolone)	0.05 0.10	09 11
BHC (BHC)	0.05 0.10	07 11
Chlordane (Termex)	0.05 0.10	11 13
Malathion (Cythion)	0.50 1.00	13 17

*Names in parenthesis are the trade/commercial names of pesticides.

ingredients are required. They are thus required to be diluted before use. Along with this the total quantity of solution required to be prepared for per unit area, must also be known. Combining all of them a formula has been outlined as:

$$d = \frac{a \times b}{c}$$

Where,

a = Percentage concentration of the pesticide desired.

b = Quantity of the solution/dust required for application.

c = Percentage of active ingredient available in the commercial pesticide/formulation.

d = Quantity of the commercial formulation required to be used.

For example percentage of Dimethoate solution to be used = 0.1 per cent ...(*a*)

Quantity of solution required to be prepared for application = 200 litres ...(*b*)

Percentage of active ingredient in the commercial pesticide = 30 per cent EC ...(*c*)

Then "*d*" or the quantity of the commercial pesticide required to be used will be:

$$\frac{0.1 \times 200}{30} = 0.66 \text{ litres or 666 ml.}$$

Weight or volume of diluent = (quantity of solution required-quantity of Commercial pesticide required)

= (200-0.666) = 199.334 litres.

Therefore, to obtain 200 litres of 0.1 per cent Dimethoate from Dimethoate 30 per cent EC (commercial formulation), 0.666 litre (666 ml) of Dimethoate 30 per cent EC should be added to 199.334 litres of water.

(vi) Application techniques: Effective spraying or dusting are skilled jobs and hence must be planned well in advance of execution. This includes prevention of waste, uniform coverage of the target and avoiding hazards to the operator. Guidelines for effective and safe use of insecticides includes precautionary measures that have to be followed prior to application (identification of the pest, symptoms, selection of insecticide, application equipment must be kept ready, informing the neighbour farmers regarding the application programme), while diluting (wearing protective devices, keeping away the children, avoid splashing while pouring the liquid solutions, never eat/drink/smoke, persons with sours and open wounds should never be allowed to carryout this work), during application (no application in the hot hours, apply dusts in early morning, don't blow clogged nozzles or hoses with mouth, under leaf coverage should be ensured) and after application (clean the equipment, destroy empty containers, keep unused pesticides safely out of the reach of children and pet animals, wash hands and body). Harvest of mulberry leaf for feeding to silkworms followed by application of insecticides should be undertaken strictly after the safe period indicated with each recommendation to avoid loss of silkworm crop due to residual toxic effect of applied insecticides.

(vii) Biological control of mulberry pests: Mulberry is prone to the attack of wide range of pests. Of them mealy bug, thrips and whitefly occupies the major status. Repeated use of pesticides not only develops resistance in the pests against the pesticides, but also leaves the chances of detrimental and other hazardous effects on silkworm, human being and ecosystem. Moreover, in some cases the pesticide spray may not hit the target insect because of their habit, habitat and body adaptations. As biological control was already proved as living weapon over chemical control, efforts were made to find out the bio-control agents in this ecosystem, which resulted in discovery of wide range of native predators for all major pests. Amongst these a promising native predator of mealy bug and leaf roller has been identified and ready reckoner for these prepared and presented next page (Table 4.4).

Table 4.3 : List of Pesticides/pesticide Formulations Banned in India

A. Pesticides banned for manufacture, import and use (24 Nos.)	
Aldrin	Benzene hexachloride
Calcium cyanide	Chlordane
Copper acetoarsenite	Clbromochloropropane
Endrin	Ethyl mercury chloride
Ethyl parathion	Heptachlor
Menazone	Nitrofen
Paraquat dimethyl sulphate	Pentachloro nitrobenzene
Pentachlorophenol	Sodium methane arsonate
Tetradifon	Toxafen
Aldicarb	Chlorobenzilate
Dieldrine	Maleic hydrazide
Ethylene dibromide	TCA (Trichloro acetic acid)
B. Pesticide/pesticide formulations banned for use but their manufacture is allowed for export (3 Nos.)	
Nicotin sulphate	Phenyl mercury acelate
Captafol 80 per cent powder	
C. Pesticide formulations banned for import, manufacture and use (4 Nos.)	
Methomyl 24 per cent L	Methomyl 12.5 per cent L
Phosphamidon 85 per cent SL	Carbofuron 50 per cent SP

Table 4.4: Ready Reckoner for Biological Control (Govindaiah *et al.*, 2005)

S.N.	Name of the pest	Name of the biological control agents	Release rate/ acre
1.	Mealy bug	*Cyrptolaemus montrouzieri,* *Scymnus coccivora*	250 500
2.	Leaf roller	*Trichogramma chilionis,* *Tetrastichus howaedii*	1 lakh 1 lakh
3.	Bihar hairy caterpillar	*Trichogramma chilionis*	1 lakh

Mass Production of Egg Parasitoid *Trichogramma Chilionis*

Trichogramma chilionis (Hymenoptera - Trichogrammatidae) is a tiny black parasitoid, which laid their eggs inside the eggs of Leaf roller and Bihar hairy caterpillar. On hatching they start eating the developing caterpillar inside the egg. A parasitoid caterpillar becomes black in colour and the young wasp develops inside it. After 8-10 days inside the host egg, the young *Trichogramma* parasitoid emerges as an adult. The adult female wasp survives for 5-14 days and can parasitise up to 50 moth eggs.

Procedure for Fiel d Release

The rationale of inundate release is that at certain periods, due to biotic and/or abiotic factors, the natural enemy population declines to a great extent, resulting in inadequate control; artificial releases during such critical periods would strengthen the population of natural enemies in abating the pest. The idea is to tilt rapidly the ratio of pest to predator in favour of the latter, thus preventing serious damage. In other words, the primary aim of inundate releases is to outnumber the pest population to bring about its immediate control without any expectations of long-term regulation, as in classical biological control. Thus, repeated releases, with the application of chemical pesticides, might be necessary. Therefore, mass production of natural enemies is an essential pre-requisite for such programmes.

(*a*) The predators are released over the entire infested area to obtain more uniform and effective control.

(*b*) Since the farmers are not familiar with handling, releasing and also the exact role of predators, it is necessary that experts should supervise the field release programme.

(*c*) The predators have to be released generally during evening hours, so that they can settle on the mealy bug colonies overnight. The required number of predators have to be assessed depending upon the area of mulberry field (Santha Kumar *et al.*, 2000).

Integrated Pest Management (IPM)

Integrated Pest Management (IPM) is a system, which utilizes all suitable pest suppression techniques in cost effective, environmental friendly and compatible manners in order to keep or maintain the pest population below those causing economic injury. The main objective of IPM is as follows:

(*a*) IPM is a broad ecological pest control approach aiming at best mix of all known pest control measures to keep the pest population below Economic Threshold Level (ETL).

(*b*) It is an economically justified and sustainable system of crop protection that leads to maximum productivity with the least possible adverse impact on the total environment.

(*c*) It is a schedule of practices, which starts from field selection till harvest of a crop. The major components in this approach are cultural, mechanical, biological and chemical methods of insect pests, diseases, weeds etc in a compatible manner.

Central Silk Board is playing a leading role in popularisation of IPM technology among the farming sericulture community. The main activity is:

(*i*) Popularising IPM approach among farming community.

(*ii*) Organizing regular pest surveillance and monitoring to assess pest/disease situation and study agro-eco-system to advise timely IPM control measures.

(*iii*) Rearing biological control agents for their field use and conservation of naturally occurring biological control agents for control of crop pests.

(*iv*) Promoting use of neem based pesticides, *bacillus* based bio-pesticides, insect pathogen as alternative to chemical pesticides.

(*v*) To play a catalytic role in transfer of innovative IPM skills/methods/techniques to extension workers and farmers in all silk producing states.

(*vi*) To preserve eco-system and environment.

(*vii*) Human Resource Development (HRD) in IPM by imparting training to officers, extension workers and farmers.

(*viii*) Field releases of laboratory reared bio-control agents for the control of pests.

(*ix*) Issuing insect-pest and disease situation bulletins for the benefit of State functionaries and farmers.

Following steps are taken in implementing the IPM technology:

- Assessment of knowledge, attitude and practice of farmers.
- Identification of major pests problems responsible for low yield.
- Deep summer ploughing.
- Collection and destruction of crop residues, weeds etc.
- Growing pest and disease resistant/tolerant varieties.
- Optimum plant spacing.
- Balanced use of fertilizers.
- Proper water management.
- Timely weed control.
- Use of light, yellow, sticky and pheromone traps.
- Regular monitoring on pests and their natural enemies.
- Conservation of crop defenders (parasites, predators and pathogens).
- Augmentation of crop defenders by release of egg, pupal, larval parasites and predators.
- Use of bio-pesticides against crop pests.

- Collection of egg-masses and larvae for their destruction.
- Need based and judicious use of the pesticides on the basis of ETL as a last resort.

IPM has been developed against the major mulberry pests (Govindaiah *et al.*, 2005) which is summarized below:

(a) IPM for mealy bug

- Clipping and destruction of tukra infested apical portion of mulberry.
- Spraying 0.2 per cent DDVP (2.63 ml in one litre of water) twice at interval of 10 days. Safe period for feeding mulberry leaves to silkworm larvae is 17 days after spraying DDVP.
- Release of predatory beetles, *Cryptolaemous montrouzieri* @ 250 adults/acre or *Scymnus coccivora* @ 500 adults/acre. It leads 70 per cent suppression in tukra infestation at farmers' level.

(b) IPM for leaf roller

- Clipping and destroying the infested parts of mulberry plant.
- Foliar spray of 0.076 per cent DDVP 76 per cent EC (1 ml in one litre of water) 10 days after pruning/leaf harvest and to be repeated at an interval of one week (if the infestation is severe). The leaf can be utilized for silkworm rearing 7 days after last application of DDVP.
- Release of an egg parasitoid *Trichogramma chilionis* @ 1 lakh adults per acre in 4 equal splits and a pupal parasitoid, *Tetrastichus howardii* @ 1 lakh per acre.

(c) IPM for Bihar hairy caterpillar

- Collection and destruction of egg masses and gregarious young caterpillars.
- Foliar application of 0.15 per cent DDVP with a waiting period of 10 days.

- Release of egg parasitoid, *Trichogramma chilionis* @ 2.5 lakh adults per hectare (12-13 trichocards) between 25th and 30th day after pruning/previous leaf harvest.

(II) DISEASE FORECASTING

Disease forecasting *i.e.* the prediction of disease outbreak and its status of severity well in advance is an important measure for improving disease control decision. It also ensures appropriate control measures in preventing economic damage at the correct time for maximum effectiveness. This prediction is possible by studying the influence of biotic and abiotic environmental interference on the population of pathogen in the population of host (Kranz, 1974). Van der Plank (1963) has formulated various equations for calculating disease epidemics in plants. These equations are used for developing forecasting models and that required accurate data on the interaction of all factors with host, pathogen and environment and their correct interpretation. Accordingly, disease assessments are made over a period of time to get reflection of disease spread in plant population. From the information obtained, infection rate (r) of pathogen is estimated to incorporate in the equation of epidemics as it fits.

(a) Infection Rate: Infection rate (r) of a given pathogen is calculated after determining the life cycle pattern *i.e.* whether the pathogen is monocyclic or polycyclic. The monocyclic pathogens complete a part or all of its life cycle in one season. Many soil borne pathogens are in this group, and usually restricted to one generation per season. The infection rate in this case, is being calculated based on the formula as indicated below:

$$r = \frac{2.3}{t_2 - t_1} \log 10 \frac{1 - x_1}{1 - x_2}$$

Where x_1 and x_2 are the proportion of the disease at the time t_1 and t_2 respectively.

Polycyclic pathogens, on the other hand, increase in host population logarithmically against time. Most of the foliar pathogens are in this group. Hence, the infection rate (r), which is called 'exponential infection rate' or 'apparent rate of infection', is calculated based on the assumption that the disease will multiply through several successive generations in course of an epidemic. For this the following equation can be used:

$$r = \frac{2.3}{t_2 - t_1} \log 10 \frac{x_2 (1 - x_1)}{x_1 (1 - x_2)}$$

Where x_1 and x_2 are the proportions of disease at the time t_1 and t_2 respectively.

(b) Model for disease forecasting: A large number of equations have been formulated from time to time to forecast diseases in various crop plants, and as the time advanced, the earlier equations are modified with the use of complicated statistical methods in making perfection in forecast systems. Relatively, recently a few of the important equations are used in preparation of models for both short-term and long-term disease forecast separately, which can also be used effectively for disease forecasting in mulberry.

(i) Short-term disease forecast: Short-term disease forecasting is done during or just before the crop season to monitor a disease during the course of plant growth. This requires initial status of disease or inoculum density at field level either by calculating proportion of disease intensity or by measuring the quantum of inoculum with its infection efficiency.

Forecasting Models for Monocyclic Diseases

The disease caused by monocyclic pathogen increases on the initial amount of inoculum, since, the pathogen does not produce effective inoculum during the growing season of the plants. Accordingly, the forecasting can be made based on the initial disease study by using the formula indicated below:

$$x_t = x_0 rt \text{ (Fry, 1982)}$$

Where x_t and x_0 are the proportion of disease at the time 't' and '0' (initial) and 'r' is the infection rate in respect of x_t. In the other way, if the inoculum (Q) and its infection efficiency (R) are considered for the study, then 'x_0', and 'r' are to be substituted by 'Q' and 'R' respectively, and the above formula can be written as:

$$x_t = \text{QRt (Fry, 1982)}$$

The quantum of inoculum in the above formula can be measured by counting sclerotia, spores etc., while, 'R' by the formula furnished below:

$$R = r\frac{x_t}{x_{t-p}} \text{ (Manner, 1982)}$$

Where 'p' is the latent period of infection, x_t the proportion of susceptible issue infected at time t, x_{t-p} the proportion which was infected at time $t - p$ and which is infectious at time t, and 'r' the rate of infection in respect of x_t. Disease forecasting with the use of inoculum quantum will be very effective when climatic conditions will remain favourable all along to form an epidemic and sufficient number of hosts will be present (Shrum, 1978 and Fry, 1982).

Forecasting Models for Polycyclic Diseases

Disease development by polycyclic pathogens depends on both the amount of initial inoculum and characteristic rate of exponential increase of particular pathogen (Fry, 1982). Accordingly, Van der Plank (1963) has formulated an equation for measuring an exponential growth of disease, which is being used frequently in disease forecasting. The formula is as follows:

$$x = x_0 e^{rt}$$

Where 'x' and x_0 are the proportion of the disease at time 't' and '0' (initial) respectively, 'e' the natural logarithm, as before, 'r' the apparent rate of infection and 't' the time period during which host and pathogen have to interact. Otherwise, if sporulation study is considered as the basis of forecasting the disease, then the equation developed by Blackman (1979) may be used for foliar diseases with certain modification by considering the amount of inoculum as disease intensity:

$$x = \text{In } x_0 + rt \text{ (Blackman, 1919)}$$

Where, the symbol 'In' is the natural logarithm to the base 'e' while 'x' and 'x_0' the amounts of inoculum (considered as disease intensity) at the time 't' and '0' (initial), respectively, 'r' the relative rate of sporulation and 't' the time period.

(ii) Long-term disease forecast: Long-term disease forecast, *i.e.* prediction of a disease a year or several years in advance. This system does not require any study on initial disease status or quantum of inoculum like in short-term. In this case disease intensity is considered as dependent variable on environmental factors. There, a relationship is established between the disease statuses and simultaneous environmental conditions viz., temperature, relative humidity, rainfall, sunshine period, wind speed, dewfall etc. (as abiotic) and aphids, beetle, leafhopper, white fly etc. (biotic-vector pest), collected regularly over a long-period of time to include every possible variations.

Most commonly linear regression is used for disease forecasting (Hori, 1963 and Kim, 1982). At first step, all the independent variables (abiotic factors) are analysed separately by the standard formula:

$$Y = a + bx$$

Where, 'Y' (dependent variable) is the disease status in term of disease intensity, index, 'x' (independent variable) a parameter of environmental conditions and 'a' (Y-intercept) and 'b' (slope of line) the constants resulting from the observed data:

Bibliography

Alam, M.M. (1993). Bioactivity against Phyto-nematodes; in '*Neem Research and Development*'. Randhawa, N. S. and Parmar, B. S. (eds.), pp. 123-143, Society of Pesticide Science, India.

Ashok, P. (1985). A New Approach to Sericulture Management. *Indian Silk*, **24**: 19-22

Atwal, A. S.; Singh, B. and Battu, G. S. (1973). *Chilopartellus* (Swinhoe) a new host of *Aspergillus flavus* Link and *Fusarium* sp, *Curr. Sci.*, **42**: 585.

Bakshi, B. K. and Singh, S. (1961). New and Noteworthy Records of some Mildews and Rusts on Indian trees. *Indian For.*, **87**: 542-545.

Bandyopadyay, U. K.; Das, N. K. and Saratchandra, B. (1999a). Studies on the use of Carbaryl Monocrotophos and Quinalphos for Control of Whitefly, *Dialeuropora decempuncta* Quaintance & Baker, on Mulberry, *Morus* sp. *J. Adv. Zool.*, **20**: 100-102.

Bandyopadyay, U. K.; Raina, S. K.; Chakravorthy, N.; Santha Kumar, M. V.; Sen, S. K. and Saratchandra, B. (1999b). New Record of a Homopteran Pest on Mulberry (*Morus alba*). *Sericologia*, **39**: 319-321.

Bandyopadyay, U. K. and Santha Kumar, M. V. (2000). Efficacy of some Insecticide alone and in Combination with Neem oil cake against the whitefly, *Dialeuropora decempuncta* infesting mulberry. *J. Ent. Res.*, **24**: 325-329.

Bandyopadyay, U. K. and Santha Kumar, M. V. (2003). Record of Host Plants of Whitefly, *Dialeuropora decempuncta* (Quaintance & Baker) in West Bengal. *Insect Environ.*, **8**: 177-178.

Bandyopadyay, U. K.; Sahu, P. K.; Raina, S. K.; Santha Kumar, M. V.; Chakraborty, N. and Sen, S. K. (2000). Studies on the Seasonal

Incidence of the Whitefly (*Dialeuropora decempuncta*). *Intl. J. Indust. Entomol.*, **1**: 65-71.

Bandyopadyay, U. K.; Santha Kumar, M. V.; Das, K. K. and Saratchandra, B. (2001). Yield loss in Mulberry due to Sucking pest of Whitefly, *Dialeuropora decempuncta* (Quaintance & Baker) (Homoptera: Aleyrodidae). *Intl. J. Indust. Entomol.*, **2**: 75-78.

Bandyopadyay, U. K.; Santha Kumar, M. V.; Mukherjee, P. K. and Saratchandra, B. (2002). Determination of Economic Threshold Level of Whitefly, *Dialeuropora decempuncta* (Quaintance & Baker) in Mulberry (*Morus alba* L.). *Intl. J. Indust. Entomol.*, **4**: 133-136.

Belcher, J. V. and Hussey, R. S. (1977). Influence of *Tegetus patula* and *Archis hypogia* on *Meloidogyne incognita. Plant Dis. Rep.*, **61**: 527-528.

Bhagyrathy, N.; Siddappaji, C.; Shankar, M. A.; Chinnaswamy, K. P. and Chavan, S. (2000). Interaction of Root Knot Nematode, *Meloidogyne incognita* and fungus *Rhizoctonia bataticola* on Mulberry plants; in *'Moriculture in Tropics'* Chinnaswamy, K. P.; Govindan, R.; Krishna Prasad, N. K. and Reddy, D. N. R. (eds.), pp. 152-153, University of Agricultural Sciences, GKVK, Bangalore, India.

Bhattacharjee, S. S.; Chakraborthy, N.; Kumar, C. A. and Sahakundu, A. K. (1994). Control of White Powdery mildew, *Phyllactinia corylea* (Pers.) with the Ladybird beetle, *Illeis indica* (Coccinellidae: Coleoptera). *Sericologia*, **34**: 485-491.

Bhatti, D. S. and Walia, R. K. (1992). *Nematode Pests of Crops*. CBS Publishers and Distributors, Delhi, p. 381.

Bheemanna, C.; Hiremath, P. C.; Palakshappa, M. G. and Govindan, R. (1990). Powdery Mildew of Mulberry and its Control. *Indian Silk*, **29**: 43-44.

Biradar, N. (1989). Faunistic Study of Arthropods Infesting Mulberry and biology of *Euproctis fraterna* (Moore). M.Sc. (Seric.) Thesis, UAS, Bangalore, p.81.

Biswas, S. and Pavan Kumar, T. (1995). *Pseudocercospora mori:* Mulberry leaf spot fungus. *Indian Silk*, **34**: 19-20.

Biswas, S.; Das, D.; Das, S. K. and Das, N. K. (2001). Incidence of Red Rust in Darjeeling hills of West Bengal. *Indian J. Seric.*, **40**: 177-179.

Biswas, S.; Das, N. K. and Pavan Kumar, T. (1996). Influence of host genotypes, Shoot age and climatic conditions on the Development of *Pseudocercospora mori* in Mulberry. *Sericologia*, **36**: 737-742.

Biswas, S.; Das, N. K.; Quadri, S. M. H. and Saratchandra, B. (1995). Evaluation of Different Plant extracts against Three Major Diseases of Mulberry. *Indian Phytopathol.*, **48**: 342-346.

Biswas, S., Mandal, S. K. and Chinya, P. K. (1993). Development of Powdery Mildew Disease in Mulberry and its Control. *Sericologia,* **33**: 653-662.

Biswas, S., Mandal, S. K., Teotia, R. S., Nair, B. P. and Sengupta, K. (1995). Intensity of Powdery Mildew in West Bengal with some Measures to Control. *Indian J. Seric.,* **34**: 114-117.

Biswas, S.; Sen, S. K. and Pavan Kumar, T. (1995). Integrated Disease Management System in Mulberry. *Sericologia,* **35**: 401-415.

Biswas, S.; Rao, A.A.; Mandal, S.K. and Rao, B.N. (1992). Influence of Diurnal Variations and Climatic Conditions on the Conidial Dispersal of *Phyllactinia corylea. Indian J. Seric.,* **31**: 135-139.

Blackmann, V. H. (1919). The Compound Interest Law and Plant Growth. *Ann. Bot.* (London), **33**: 353-360.

Chandrashekar, D.S.; Shehar Shetty H. and Datta, R.K. (1997). Effect of VAM fungi, *Glomus fasciculatum* and *Acaulospora laevis,* against the Root Knot Nematode of Mulberry. *Sericologia,* **37**: 105-108.

Chatterjee, S. N. and Raychoudhuri, S. P. (1965). A Note on Aphid Transmission of Mosaic Disease of Mulberry. *Indian Phytopathol.,* **18**: 19-20.

Chaudhary, S. K. and Raj, S. K. (1986). *Fusarium solani* (Mart). A New Pathogen Causing Leaf Spot Disease in Mulberry and its Control. *Sericologia,* **26**: 125-130.

Chen, J.Y. (1995). A Study on Mulberry Mosaic Disease. *Acta Sericologia Sinica* (*Canye Kexue*), **21**: 9-14.

Chitra, C.; Karanth, N. G. K. and Vasantharajan, V. N. (1975). Diseases of the Mulberry Silkworm, *Bombyx mori* L. *J. Sci. Indust. Res.,* **34**: 386-401.

Chowdary, N. P.; Govindaiah and Sharma, D. D. (2003). Microbial Complexity of Mulberry (*Morus* spp.) Root Rot Disease in South India; in *'Plant Pathogens Diversity in Relation to Plant Health',* Manoharachary, C. (ed.); p. 112, Osmania University, Hyderabad, India.

Damicone, J. P.; Conway, K. E. and Moter, J. E. (2002). Anthracnose and other Common Leaf Diseases of Deciduous Shade Trees. *Oklahoma Co-operative Extension Service, OSU Extension facts,* F. 7634.

Das, C.; Shivanath and Rao, K. M. (1994). An Investigation on Morphological Changes due to Thrips Infesting Mulberry, *Morus alba* L. *Geobios,* **21**: 109-113.

Datta, S. K. (1981). Scale Insect Fauna of the World. Part–I. Armored scales. Seminar Report, UAS, Bangalore, p.44.

Dhar, A.; Raina, S. K. and Ahsan, M. M. (1988). A New Fungal Report on Mulberry from India. *Int. J. Trop. Pl. Dis.*, **6**: 273-274.

Ertian, H. (2003). *Protection of Mulberry Plants* (Translated from Chinese), Oxford and IBH Publishing, Co. Pvt. Ltd., New Delhi, India.

Fry, W. E. (1982). *Principles of Plant Disease Management*. Academic Press, New York.

Geethabai, M.; Marimadaiah, B.; Narayanaswamy, K. C. and Rajagopal, D. (1997). An Outbreak of Leaf Roller Pest, *Diaphania* (= *Margoronia*) *pulverulentalis* (Hampson) on Mulberry in Karnataka. *Geobios New Reports*, **19**: 73-79.

Ghosh, S. K. (1972). Biology of the Mealy Bug, *Maconellicoccus hirsutus* (Green) (Pseudococcidae: Hemiptera). *Indian J. Agric.*, **16**: 323-332.

Govindaiah (1990). Studies on Root Knot Nematode, *Meloidogyne incognita* infesting Mulberry. Ph. D. Thesis, University of Mysore, Mysore, India.

Govindaiah and Bhakuni, B. C. (1988). Prevalence of Tukra Disease in Tropical Regions. *Indian Silk*, **26**: 55.

Govindaiah and Sharma, D.D. (1994). Root-knot Nematode, *Meloidogyne incognita* Infesting Mulberry - A review. *Indian J. Seric.*, **33**: 110-113.

Govindaiah; Dandin, S. B. and Madhavarao, Y. R. (1988). Host Range of *Meloidogyne incognita* causing Root Knot in Mulberry (*Morus alba* L.). *Indian J. Seric.*, **28**: 121-126.

Govindaiah; Dandin, S. B. and Sharma, D. D. (1991). Pathogenicity and Avoidable Leaf Yield Loss due to *Meloidogyne incognita* in Mulberry (*Morus alba* L.) *Indian J. Nematol.*, **21**: 52-57.

Govindaiah; Dandin, S. B.; Giridhar, K. and Datta, R.K. (1994). Efficacy of Different doses of Neem oil cake on *Meloidogyne incognita* Infesting mulberry. *Sericologia*, **34**: 717-721.

Govindaiah; Gupta, V. P.; Sharma, D. D.; Rajadurai, S. and Nishitha Naik, V. (2005) "*Mulberry Crop Protection*" published by Central Silk Board, Bangalore, pp. 459.

Govindaiah; Gunasekhar, V.; Gowda, P. and Thiagarajan, V. (1994). Field Evaluation of Fungicide against *Phyllactinia corylea* Causing Powdery Mildew in Mulberry (*Morus alba* L.). *Indian J. Seric.*, **33**: 160-162.

Govindaiah; Sengupta, K.; Sharma, D. D.; Gargi and Gunasekhar, V. (1989 b). A New Leaf Spot Disease of Mulberry caused by *Myrothecium roridum*. *Current Science*, **58**: 398.

Govindaiah; Sharma, D. D.; Gunasekhar, V. and Datta, R.K. (1996). Screening of Mulberry Genotypes against Root Knot Nematode Disease (*Meloidogyne incognita*). *Indian J. Nematology*, **26**: 108-111.

Govindaiah; Sharma, D. D.; Hemantharaj, M. T. and Bajpai, A. K. (1997). Nematicidal Efficacy of Organic Manures, Intercrops, Mulches and Nematicide against Root Knot Nematode in Mulberry. *Indian J. Nematol.*, **27**: 28-35.

Govindaiah; Sharma, D. D.; Singal, B.K. and Sengupta, K. (1990). *Fusarium Pallidoroserum* (Cooke) Sacc - A New Pathogen causing Leaf Blight in Mulberry (*Morus alba* L.). *Indian J. Seric.*, **29**: 291-292.

Govindaiah; Philip, T.; Sengupta, K.; Giridhar, K. and Suryanarayana, N. (1990a). Incidence of Leaf Spot Disease in some Indigenous varieties of Mulberry. *Sericologia*, **30**: 257-260.

Govindaiah; Sharma, D. D.; Choudhury, P. C.; Mallikarjuna, B. and Madhavarao, Y. R. (1990b). Incidence of Fungal Diseases of Mulberry under Different Agronomical Practices. *Sericologia*, **30**: 237-242.

Govindaiah; Sharma, D. D.; Singhal, B. K. and Sengupta, K. (1990c). *Fusarium pallidoroseum* - A New Pathogen causing Leaf Blight in mulberry. *Indian J. Seric.*, **29**: 291-292.

Gowda Sidde, D. K.; Manjunath, D.; Kumar, P. and Datta, R. K. (1995). Termites in Mulberry Plantations. *Indian Silk*, **34**: 29-30.

Gunasekhar, V.; Govindaiah and Datta, R. K. (1992). A New Leaf Blight of Mulberry (*Morus* spp.) caused by *Alternaria alternata* in India. *Indian J. Seric.*, **31**: 131-134.

Gunasekhar, V.; Govindaiah and Datta, R. K. (1994). Occurrence of *Alternaria* Leaf Blight of Mulberry and a key for Disease Assessment. *Internat. J. Tropical Plant Dis.*, **12**: 53-57.

Gunasekhar, V.; Govindaiah and Himantharaj, M.T. (1995). Efficacy of fungicides in controlling leaf rust caused by *Cerotelium fici*. *Indian J. Seric.*, **34**: 60-62.

Gunasekhar, V.; Philip, T.; Govindaiah; Sharma, D. D.; Nagaraj, B. and Data, R. K. (1994). Seasonal Occurrence of Foliar, Fungal and Bacterial Diseases of Mulberry in South India. *Indian Phytopathol.*, **47**: 72-76.

Gupta, P. C. and Deng, J. K. (1983). A New Leaf Spots Disease of Mulberry (*Morus alba* L.). *Current Science*, **52**: 487-488.

Gupta, V. P. (1998). Nursery - Guard: A Biofungicide for Nursery management. *Indian Silk*, **36**: 8-9.

Gupta, V. P. (1999). On the Occurrence of Mosaic Disease on Mulberry in India. *Indian Phytopathol.*, **52**: 154-155.

Gupta, V.P. (2001) Diseases of Mulberry and their Management. In '*Plant Pathology*' (Trivedi, P.C., ed.), Pointer Publishers, Jaipur, India, pp. 130-164.

Gupta, V.P.; Govindaiah and Datta, R.K. (1994). *Fusarium moniliforme* var. *intermedium* and *F. oxysporum*: New Pathogens causing Leaf Blight and Leaf Spot in Mulberry. *Internat. J. Tropical Plant Dis.*, **12**: 101-105.

Gupta, V.P.; Sharma, D.D.; Govindaiah and Chandrashekar, D.S. (1999). Soil Solarization for the Control of Nursery Diseases in Mulberry. *Indian J. Seric.*, **38**: 44-47.

Hori, M. (1963). Studies on the Forecasting of Rice Blast with Special Reference to the Experimental Forecasting. *Spec. Res. Rep. Dis. and Ins. Forec. Min. Agr. Forest, Japan*, **14**: 1-76.

Ishijima, T. (1980). Mulberry dwarf Disease - Its Ecology and Control. Seric. Expt. Stn., Kyushu Branch, 104-115.

Itoi, S.; Nakayama, K. and Kubomura, Y. (1960). Studies on the Powdery Mildew of Mulberry tree, Caused by *Phyllactinia corylea* (Pers.) Karst (1) on the Outbreak and Subsequent Development of the Disease. *J. Sericult. Sci. Japan*, **29**: 72-74.

Kariappa, B. K. and Narasimhanna, M. N. (1981). Studies on the Life History of Wingless Grasshopper, *Neorthacris acuticeps nilgriensis* (Uvarov) (Acrididae: Orthoptera)—a Pest of Mulberry. *Indian J. Seric.*, **21**: 27-30.

Katiyar, R. L.; Manjunath, D.; Kumar, V. and Datta, R. K. (2001).Integrated Management of the Pink Mealy Bug, *Maconellicoccus hirsutus* (Green) (Hemiptera: Pseudococcidae) causing Tukra in Mulberry. *Intl. J. Indust. Entomol.*, **3**: 117-120.

Khan, M.A.; Bhat, M.M. and Singh, T. (2011). *Silkworm Crop Protection – Concepts and Approaches.* Daya Publishing House, New Delhi, pp. 224.

Kim, C. K. (1982). Improved Methods of Rice Blast Forecasting. *Korean J. Pl. Prot.*, **21**: 19-22.

Kotikal, Y. K. (1982). Studies on the Pest of Mulberry with Special Reference to the Black-headed hairy Caterpillar, *Spilosoma obliqua* (Walker). M. Sc. (Agric.) Thesis, UAS, Bangalore.

Koul, A.; Devi, S. P. and Singh, D. (1991). On the Occurrence of Yellow Net Vein Sisease on Mulberry. *Indian Phytopathol.*, **44**: 106-107.

Kranj, J. (1974). The role and scope of mathematical analysis and modelling in epidemiology; in "*Epidermis of Plant Disease: Mathematical Analysis and Modelling*, J. Kranz (ed.) pp. 7-54, Springer-Verlag, Berlin and New York.

Krishna Prasad, K. S. and Siddaramaiah, A. K. (1978). Bacterial Leaf Blight of Mulberry in Karnataka. *Indian J. Seric.*, **17**: 61-63.

Krishna Prasad, K. S. and Siddaramaiah, A. K. (1979). Studies on the Dcevelopment of Powdery Mildew Disease of Mulberry in Karnataka. *Indian J. Seric.*, **18**: 9-13.

Kumar, N. N. U. (1991). Effect of Mosaic Virus on Physiology of Mulberry (*Morus alba* L.). *Adv. Plant Sci.*, **4**: 183-185.

Kumar Narendra, J.B.; Shekhar, M.A. and Qadri, S.M.H. (2011). Giant African Snail in Mulberry: Physiology and Management. *Indian Silk*, **49**(12): 4-5.

Kumar, P. M.; Maji, M. D.; Gangwar, S. K.; Das, N. K. and Saratchandra, B. (2000). Development of leaf rust (*Psridiospora mori*) and Dispersal of Gredospores in Mulberry (*Morus* spp.). *International J. Pest Management*, **45**: 25-31.

Latha, J.; Govindaiah and Datta, R. K. (1993). In-vitro effect of culture filtrate of *Trichoderma* species against *Fusarium pallidoroseum* causing leaf blight in Mulberry. *Indian J. Seric.*, **32**: 121-123.

Lee, H. N.; Lee, K. Y.; Kim, T. J.; Sin, S. B.; Cho, J. S. and Kwon, S. I. (1992). Insecticidal Characterization of thirteen *Bacillus thuringiensis* Strains from Soil. *Korean J. Microbiol.*, **30**: 438-443.

Luke, P. B. and Sathiya Paul, K. M. (1982). A new record of *Botryodiplodia theobromae* on *Morus alba* L. *Current Science*, **51**: 427.

Maji, M. D. and Quadri, S. M. H. (1999). Bacterial Diseases of Mulberry (*Morus* spp.). *Sericologia*, **39**: 1-7.

Maji, M. D.; Quadri, S. M. H. and Paul, S. C. (1996). Bacterial leaf Dpot Disease in Mulberry. *Indian Silk*, **35**: 11-12.

Mandal, S. K. (1993). Twig Blight and New Leaf Spot Disease of Mulberry. *Indian Silk*, **32**: 51.

Mani, M. (1989). A Review of Pink Mealy Bug, *Maconellicoccus hirsutus* (Green). *Insect Sci. Applic.*, **10**: 157-167.

Mani, M.; Thontadarya, T. S. and Singh, S. P. (1987). Record of natural enemies on the Grape Mealy Bug, *Maconellicoccus hirsutus* (Green). *Curr. Sci.*, **56**: 624 - 625.

Manners, J. G. (1982). *Principles of Plant Pathology*. Cambridge University Press, Cambridge, London.

Manjunath, T. M. (1985). *Maconellicoccus hirsutus* on grapevine. *FAO Plant Protection Bulletin*, **33**: 74.

Manjunath, D.; Ramkishor; Prasad, K. S.; Kumar, V.; Kumar, P. and Datta, R. K. (1996). Biology of the Mealy Vug, *Maconellicoccus hirsutus* (Green) causing Tukra in Mulberry. *Sericologia*, **36**: 487-491.

Mary Josepha, A.V.; Soudhaminy, P.V. and Balakrishna, R. (2011). Outbreak of Whitefly in Mulberry fields of Wayanad in Kerala. *Indian Silk*, **50(8)**: 12-13.

Mathew, H.; Beena, S. and Cherian, A. K. (1994). Bacterial Wilt of Mulberry, *Morus alba* L. incited by *Pseudomonas solanacearum* (Smith) from India. *Kerala Agric. Univ., News Letter*, **9**-11.

Mitter, J. H. and Tandon, R. N. (1937). Fungi of Allahabad, India. Part III., *Proc. Indian Acad. Sci.*, **6(B)**: 194-201.

Mukherjee, S.; Dhar, A.; Sadruddin and Mukherjee, P. (1995). *Mimastra cyanura. Indian Silk*, **34**: 11-12.

Munjal, R. L.; Lall, G. and Chona, B. L. (1959). Some *Cercospora* species from India, II. *Indian Phytopathol.*, **12**: 85-89.

Munshi, N. A.; Nissar, T.; Zargar, M. A. and Das, B. C. (1986). New Leaf Spot Disease of Mulberry. *Sci. Cult.*, **52**: 238-239.

Murthy, N. C. V. (1986). Root knot Nematode Disease of Mulberry and its Control measures. *Indian Silk*, **34**: 6-8.

Naik, S. L. (1997). *Bio-ecology of Thrips Infesting Mulberry*. M.Sc. Thesis, UAS, Bangalore, p. 77.

Nair, R. R. and Premkumar, T. (1974). *Aspergillus flavus* Link, a parasite on the Leaf Eating Caterpillar, *Lymantria obfuscata* Wlk. *Current Science*, **45**: 563.

Narayanan, E. S.; Kashiviswanathan, K. and Iyengar, M. N. S. (1966). A Note on the Occurrence of Root knot Nematode, *Meloidogyne incognita* (Kofoid and White) in Local Mulberry. *Indian J. Seric.*, **5**: 33-34.

Nath, T. N.; Shivanath; Chakraborthy, N. G. and Sen, S. K. (1994). Studies on the Extent of Mulberry leaf Destruction by the Bihar hairy Caterpillar, *Diacrisia obliqua* Walker. *Sericologia*, **34**: 545-550.

Nishitha Naik, V.; Sharma, D. D.; Govindaiah and Chowdary, N. B. (2003). Occurrence of Root knot Disease complex in Mulberry due to Nematode and Fungal Association; in '*Disease and Pest Management in Sericulture*' Govindan, R. (ed.), p. 7, Sericulture College, Chintamani, India.

Nishitha Naik, V.; Sharma, D.D.; Mala, V.R. and Chowdary, N.B. (2008). Prediction of Leaf Spot Disease in Mulberry. *Indian Silk*, **47**: 7.

Oda, T. (1963) Studies on the Dispersion of the Mulberry Scale. *Jap. J. Ecol.*, **13**: 41-46.

Pandey, P. C. and Singh, S. (1989). Three Important Diseases of Mulberry in India. *Indian J. Forest.*, **12**: 255-258.

Pandotra, U. R. (1966). Notes on Fungi of Jammu & Kashmir. *Proc. Indian Acad. Sci.*, **54**: 68.

Patel, M. K.; Kamath, M. N. and Bhide, V. P. (1949). Fungi of Bombay Supplement, I. *Indian Phytopath.*, **2**: 142-155.

Paul, A.; Sinhababu, S. P. and Sukul, N. C. (1995). Effect of Nematode Infected Mulberry Plants on the Growth and Silk Production of *Bombyx mori* L. *Indian J. Seric.*, **34**: 18-21.

Philip, T. and Sharma, D.D. (1999). Antagonistic Effect of *Bacillus subtilis* on Mulberry Root rot Fungus, *Fusarium solani*. *Sericologia*, **39**: 269-272.

Philip, T.; Govindaiah and Datta, R. K. (1992). Preinfectional Structural Defense Mechanism in Mulberry against *Cercospora moricola* (Cooke) causing leaf spot. *Proc. National Conference on Mulberry Sericulture*, CSR&TI, Mysore, India (Abs. 59-60).

Philip, T.; Govindaiah,; Bajpai, A. K. and Datta, R. K. (1994). Chemical Control of Mulberry Diseases - A review. *Indian J. Seric.*, **33**: 1-5.

Philip, T.; Gupta, V. P.; Govindaiah,; Bajpai, A. K. and Datta, R. K. (1994). Diseases of Mulberry in India - Research Priorities and Management Strategies. *Int. J. Tropical Plant Diseases*, **12**: 1-21.

Philip, T.; Latha, J.; Govindaiah; Mallikarjuna, B.; Mandal, K.C. and Bajpai, A.K. (1995). Some Observation on Incidence, Associated Microflora and Control of Root rot Disease of Mulberry in South India. *Indian J. Seric.*, **34**: 137-139.

Philip, T.; Sharma, D. D. and Govindaiah (1996). Biochemical Control of Mulberry Root rot disease. *Indian Silk*, **34**: 6-8.

Pillai, V. S. (1968a). Bionomics of the *Eupterote mollifera* (Eupterotidae: Lepidoptera) - A Pest of Mulberry Plant. *Indian J. Seric.*, **7**: 52-55.

Pillai, V. S. (1968b). Studies on the Bionomics of the *Ceryx godarti* Bdv. (Syntomidae: Lepidoptera). *Indian J. Seric.*, **7**: 74-78.

Pillai, V. S. (1968c). Observation on the *Euproctis fraternal* (M.) (Lymantridae: Lepidoptera) - A Pest of Mulberry Plant in Mysore. *Indian J. Seric.*, **7**: 45 - 47.

Pillai, V. S. and Jolly, M. S. (1980). Studies on the Build-up and Control Measures of the Red Spider Mite, *Tetranychus equitorius*. *Indian J. Seric.*, **19**: 15-21.

Pillai, V. S. and Krishnaswamy, S. (1983). Population of Mulberry Thrips, *Pseudodendrothrips mori* (Nawa) in relation to Weather Parameters. *Indian J. Seric.*, **22**: 46-52.

Prasad, K. S. K. and Siddaramaiah, A. L. (1978). Studies on the Bacterial Leaf Blight of Mulberry in Karnataka. *Indian J. Seric.*, **17**: 61-63.

Prasad, K. S. K. and Siddaramaiah, A. L. (1979). Studies on the Development of Powdery Mildew Disease of Mulberry in Karnataka. *Indian J. Seric.*, **18**: 9-13.

Prasad, K. V.; Dayakar Yadav, B. R. and Sullia, S. B. (1999). Screening of Mulberry Varieties for Resistance to Leaf Rust caused by *Peridiospora mori*. *Sericologia*, **39**: 77-90.

Quadri, S. M. H.; Pratheesh Kumar, P. M.; Gangwar, S. K.; Elangovan, C.; Maji, M. D. and Saratchandra, B. (1998). Crop Loss Assessment due to Powdery Mildew in Mulberry. *Bull. Seric. Res.*, **9**: 31-35.

Quadri, S. M. H.; Ravindra, R.J.; Shekhar, M.A. and Shylesha, A.N. (2010). Tackling Papaya Mealybug in Mulberry to Sustain Sericulture. *Indian Silk*, **49**(5&6): 4-5.

Radhakrishnan, T. S. and Sundaram, N. V. (1954). Note on some Fungi from South India – III. *Indian Phytopathol.*, **7**: 61-68.

Radhakrishnan, T. S.; Ramabadran, R. and Jayaraj, S. (1995). *Botryodiplodia* root rot - A New Disease of Mulberry. *Indian Phytopathol.*, **48**: 492.

Rajadurai, S.; Manjunath, D.; Katiyar, R. L.; Prasad, K. S.; Sen, A. K.; Shekhar, M. A.; Ahsan, M. M. and Datta, R. K. (1999). Leaf roller – A Serious Pest of Mulberry. *Indian Silk*, **37**: 9-11.

Rajadurai, S.; Bhattacharya, S. and Shekhar, M. A. (2002a). Life Table Studies of Leaf Loller, *Diaphania pulverulentalis* (Hampson) (Lepidoptera: Pyralidae) – A Major Pest of Mulberry. *Intl. J. Indust. Entomol.*, **5**: 33-36.

Rajadurai, S.; Sen, A. K.; Manjunath, D. and Datta, R. K. (2002b). Natural Enemy Fauna of Mulberry Leaf Roller, *Diaphania pulverulentalis* (Hampson) (Lepidoptera: Pyralidae) and it's potential. *Adv. Ind. Seric. Res.* (eds) Dandin, S. B. and Gupta, V. P. (Central Silk Board, publication – Bangalore), pp. 220 - 223.

Raju, H. V. (1998). Investigation on Fungal Leaf Blight Diseases of mulberry (*Morus alba* L.). Ph. D. Thesis, University of Mysore, India, 252 pp.

Ramanjaneyulu, Y.V.; Sarvamangala, H.S.; Vijayakumar, H.V. and Subrahmanyan (2011). Giant African Snail Strolls in Mulberry garden. *Indian Silk*, **49**(12): 6-8.

Ramkishor; Manjunath, D.; Kumar, P.; Kumar, V. and Datta, R. K. (1994). Bihar hairy Caterpillar and its Management. *Indian Silk*, **32**: 13 - 15.

Rangaswamy, G.; Narashimhanna, M. N.; Kashiviswanathan, K.; Sastry, C. R. and Jolly, M. S. (1976). Mulberry Cultivation. *Manual on Sericulture*, Vol. I., FAO, Publication Rome.

Rao, S.S. and Sullia, S.B. (1981). A Hyperparasite of *Phyllactinia corylea*, the Powdery Mildew of Mulberry. *Current Science*, **50**: 769.

Rao, C. H. N.; Veeranna, G. and Prasad, N. R. (1993). Studies on the Infestation of *Exorista sorbillans* on *Bombyx mori* L. - Incidence during monsoon season. *Proc. Natl. Sem. Uzi fly and its Control*, KSSRDI, Bangalore, pp. 49-56.

Raychaudhuri, S. P. and Nariani, T. K. (1977). *Virus and Mycoplasma Diseases of Plants in India*. Oxford & I.B.H. Publishing Co., New Delhi.

Raychaudhuri, S. P.; Chatterjee, S. N. and Dhar, H. K. (1961). Preliminary Note on the Occurrence of Yellow-net vein Disease of Mulberry. *Indian Phytopathol.*, **14**: 94-95.

Raychaudhuri, S. P.; Chatterjee, S. N. and Dhar, H. K. (1962). A Mosaic Disease of Mulberry. *Indian Phytopathol.*, **15**: 187-189.

Raychaudhuri, S. P.; Ganguly, B. and Basu, A. N. (1965). Studies on the Mosaic Disease of Mulberry. *Plant Dis. Rep.*, **49**: 982.

Reddy, D. N. R. and Kotikal, Y. K. (1988). Pest Infesting Mulberry and their Management. *Indian Silk*, **26**: 9-15.

Reddy, D. N. R. and Narayanaswamy, K. C. (1999a). Pest Infesting Mulberry and their Management; in "*Advances in Mulberry Sericulture*", Devaiah, M. C.; Narayanaswamy, K. C. and Mariabashetty, V. G. (eds.) (CVG Publication - Bangalore), pp. 145 - 153.

Reddy, D. N. R. and Narayanaswamy, K. C. (1999b). Pest Status of Thrips Infesting Mulberry. *Indian J. Seric.*, **38**: 1 - 7.

Reddy, M. H. and Rao, A. S. (1974). A New Leaf Spot Disease of Mulberry caused by *Fusarium concolor*. *Current Science*, **43**: 530.

Reming, D.; Juango, S. P.; Ping, M. J.; Jianan, F. and Xiaole, W. W. (1988). Studies on a New Leaf Spot Disease of Mulberry caused by *Myrothecium roridum*. *International Congress on Tropical Sericulture Practices* (Bangalore) February, 8-12, pp.1-12.

Rongsen, L. and Zhunei, S. (1993). Host Specificity of *Bacillus thuringiensis* (Delta) Endotoxin Proteolysed by Proteases of Larval Gut Juice. *Acta Entomologia Sinica*, **36**: 362-271.

Sahakundu, P. K. (1994). Population Dynamics of Mulberry Thrips in West Bengal. *Environ. Ecol.*, **12**: 356-359.

Sastry, C. R. (1984). Mulberry Varieties, Exploitation and Pathology. *Sericologia*, **24**: 333-359.

Sengupta, K.; Kumar, P.; Baig, M. and Govindaiah (1990). *Handbook on Pest and Disease Control of Mulberry and Silkworm.* Economics and Social Commission for Asia and Pacific, United Nations, Bangkok, Thailand.

Shankar, M. A. (1997). *Hand Book of Mulberry Nutrition.* Multiplex, Bangalore, pp. 121.

Sharma, D. D. (1998a). Distribution of Nematode (*Meloidogyne incognita*) population in Affected Mulberry gardens. *International J. Tropical Plant Dis.*, **16**: 73-79.

Sharma, D. D. (1998b). Eco-friendly Approach for Management of Root knot. *Indian Silk*, **37 (4):** 15-16.

Sharma, D. D. (1999a). Root knots Disease of Mulberry and its Management. *Indian Farming*, **49**: 20-24.

Sharma, D. D. (1999b). Management of Root rot Disease of Mulberry. *Indian Silk*, **37**: 11-12.

Sharma, D.D. (2008). Mulberry Leaf Spot Diseases and their Management. *Indian Silk*, **47**: 5-6.

Sharma, D.D. and Govindaiah (1991a). Influence of Agronomical Practices on Disease Occurrence in Mulberry. *Indian Silk*, **34**: 40.

Sharma, D.D. and Govindaiah (199b1). Comparative in-vitro Toxicity of Fungicides against *Pseudomonas mori* causing Bacterial Blight of mulberry. *Indian J. Seric.*, **30**: 139-140.

Sharma, D.D. and Sarkar, A. (1998). Incidence and Intensity of Species/ races of Root knot Nematode Associated with Mulberry under Different farming Systems and Soil types in Mysore Region, Karnataka State. *Indian J. Seric.*, **37**: 137-141.

Sharma, D. D.: Baqual, M. F.; Gupta, V. P. and Chandraskhar, D. S. (2000). A Survery on the Occurrence of Bacterial Blight Disease Complex in Mulberry. *Indian J. Seric.*, **39:** 113-116.

Sharma, D. D.; Chandrashekar, D. S.; Gunasekhar, V.; Rekha, M. and Sarkar, A. (2001). Comparative Efficacy of Different Control Measures against Root knot Nematode Disease of Mulberry. *Indian J. Seric.*, **40**: 151-157.

Sharma, D. D.; Chandrashekar, D. S.; Srikantaswamy, K. and Govindaiah (1998). On-form evaluation of Cultural and Chemical Methods for the Control of Root-knot Nematode Disease of Mulberry. *Indian J. Seric.*, **37**: 61-63.

Sharma, D. D.; Govindaiah; Mishra, R. K.; Choudhary, P. C.; Bajpai, A. K. and Datta, R. K. (1995). Effect of a VAM Fungi on the Incidence of Mulberry Disease in Chawki garden. *Indian J. Seric.*, **34**: 150-155.

Sharma, D. D.; Nishitha Naik, V.; Chowdary, N. B. and Mala V. R. (2003). Soil borne Diseases of Mulberry and their Management. *Int. J. Indust. Entomol.*, **7**: 93-106.

Sharma, P. D. (1974). A New Leaf Spot Disease of Mulberry in India. *Current Science*, **43**: 429.

Sharma, P. P. (1989). Insect Pest of Sericulture and their Control. *Pesticides*, **23**: 19-23.

Sharma, S.D.; Chandrasekharan K.; Nataraju, B.; Balavenkatasubbaiah, M.; Selvakumar, T.; Thiagarajan, V. and Dandin, S.B. (2003). The Cross Infectivity between Pathogens of Silkworm, *Bombyx mori* L. and Mulberry Leaf Roller, *Diaphania pulverulentalis*. *Sericologia*, **43**: 10-18.

Shree, M. P. (1984). Control of Mulberry Canker Disease caused by *Botryodiplodia theobromae*. *Sericologia*, **18**: 325-331.

Shree, M. P. and Boraiah, G. (1988). Incidence of 'Tukra' and Bacterial Blight of Mulberry plants in Germplasm Bank. *Current Science*, **57**: 1221-1228.

Shree, M. P. and Kumar, N. N. U. (1991). Changes in the Elemental Composition of Mulberry Leaves (*Morus alba* L. Var. S54) Infected by foliar Pathogens. *Sericologia*, **31**: 441-444.

Shree, M. P. and Manjunath, S. (1998). Incidence of Bihar hairy Caterpillar (*Spilarctia obliqua* Walker) in Mulberry gardens. *Indian J. Seric.*, **37**: 174 - 175.

Shrum, R. D. (1978). Forecasting of Epidermis; in "*Plant Pathology: An Advanced Treatise*", Horshfall, J. G. and Cowling, E. B. (eds.) Vol. 2, pp. 223-238, Academic Press, New York.

Siddaramaiah, A. L. and Hegde, R. K. (1988). A New Root rot, Bud and Leaf blight in Mulberry Seedlings from India. *Indian J. Seric.*, **27**: 161.

Siddaramaiah, A. L. and Hegde, R. K. (1989). Development and Severity of *Cercospora* leaf spot of mulberry in relation to environmental Factors. *Mysore J. Agric. Sci.*, **23**: 189-192.

Siddaramaiah, A. L. and Hegde, R. K. (1990). Control of Cercospora leaf spot of Mulberry: I. Evaluation of fungicides both under laboratory and in field conditions. *Mysore J. Agric. Sci.*, **24**: 327-331.

Siddaramaiah, A. L. and Patil, P. R. (1984). New Wilt Disease of Sprouted cuttings of Mulberry in Nursery from India. *Indian J. Seric.*, **23**: 46.

Siddaramaiah, A. L.; Prasad, K. S. K. and Hedge, R.K. (1978). Epidemiological Studies of Mulberry Leaf spot caused by *Cercospora moricola. Indian J. Seric.*, **17**: 44-47.

Siddaramaiah, A. L.; Padaganur, G. M.; Prasad, K. S. K. and Govindan, R. (1978). Control of Mulberry Leaf spot caused by *Cercospora moricola. Indian J. Seric.*, **17**: 23-27.

Sidde Gowda, D. K.; Gupta, V. K.; Sen, A. K.; Benchamin, K. V.; Manjunath, D.; Prasad, K. S.; Magadum, S. B. and Datta, R. K. (1995). *Diaphania* sp. Infests Mulberry in South India. *Indian Silk*, **34**: 6-8.

Sidde Gowda, D. K.; Manjunath, D.; Prasad, K. S.; Katiyar, R. L.; Kishor, R. and Datta, R. K. (1997). Natural Enemy Complex of the Pink Mulberry Crop System. *Indian J. Seric.*, **36**: 55-56.

Singh, K. (1972). Studies on the Life History and Morphology of the *Amata passalis* (Amatidae: Lepidoptera) – A Pest of Mulberry. *Indian J. Seric.*, **11**: 41- 46.

Singh, K. P. (1992). A New Mulberry Disease Caused by *Sclerotium rolfsii. Indian Phytopathol.*, **45**: 474-475.

Singh, R. and Singh, J. (1984). New Record of *Aspergillus candidus* Link, a potential Entomogenous Fungus in *Indarbela* spp. *Sci. & Cult.*, **48**: 282-283.

Singh, R.N.; Samson, M.V. and Datta, R.K. (2000). *Pest Management in Sericulture*. Indian Publishers & Distributors, New Delhi.

Singh, R.N. and Saratchandra, B. (2010). Biology of Papaya Mealybug and its Biological Control in Sericulture. *Indian Silk*, **49** (5&6): 6-7.

Singh, T. and Saratchandra, B. (2004). *Principles and Techniques of Silkworm Seed Production*. Discovery Publishing House, New Delhi, pp. 374.

Singh, T.; Bhat, M.M. and Khan, M.A. (2010). *Silkworm Egg Science – Principles and Protocols*. Daya Publishing House, New Delhi, pp. 274.

Sinha, S. K. and Saxena, S. F. (1966). First Record of Bacterial Blight of Mulberry in India caused by *Pseudomonas mori* (Boyer *et* Lambert). *Indian Phytopathol.*, **19**: 318-319.

Sreenivas, B.T.; Shekhar, M.A.; Anantharaman, K.V. and Kumar Narendra, J.B. (2011). Giant African Snail Infestation in Hoskote too. *Indian Silk*, **49**(12): 9.

Sridhar, R.; Subramanian, A. and Chandra Mohan, N. (2000). Management of Mulberry Root rot with Antagonistic Microorganisms. *Sericologia*, **40**: 383-386.

Sukumar, J. and Padma, S. D. (1999). Diseases of Mulberry in India - Research Progress and Priorities; in *'Advances in Mulberry Sericulture'*, Devaiah, M. C.; Narayanaswamy, K. C. and Maribashetty, V. G. (eds.), CVG Publications, Bangalore, pp. 155-186.

Sukumar, J. and Yadav, B.R.D. (1988). Occurrence of Leaf Blight Disease of Mulberry caused by *Fusarium lateritium* sp. *mori* Type-A in India – A new report. *Current Science*, **57**: 49-50.

Sukumar, J. and Ramalingum, A. (1989a). Antagonistic Effect of Phylopalne Microorganisms against *Cercospora moricola* Cooke. *Current Science*, **55**: 1208-1209.

Sukumar, J. and Ramalingum, A. (1989b). Epidemiology of *Cercospora* Leaf Spot Disease of Mulberry. III. Conidial Dispersal and Disease incidence. *Sericologia*, **29**: 533-539.

Sukumar, J.; Padma, S. D.; Prasad, K. V. and Bongale, U. D. (2000). Studies on some Aspects of Black Root rot Disease of Mulberry caused by *Lasiodiplodia theobromae*; in *'Moriculture in Tropics'*, Chinnaswamy, K. P.; Govindan, R.; Krishnaprasad, N. K. and Reddy, D. N. R. (eds.), pp. 121-123, University of Agricultural Sciences, GKVK, Bangalore, India.

Sukumar, J.; Yadav, B. R. D. and Prasad, K. V. (1991). Stem Canker – A Serious Nursery Disease of Mulberry in Karnataka. *Indian Silk*, **30**: 42-45.

Sullia, S. B. and Padma, S. D. (1985). *Myrothecium mori* sp. – A New Leaf Spot Pathogen of Mulberry. *Current Science*, **54**: 757-758.

Sullia, S. B. and Padma, S. D. (1987). Acceptance of Mildew Affected Mulberry leaves by Silkworm (*Bombyx mori* L.) and its Effect on Cocoon Characteristics. *Sericologia*, **27**: 693-696.

Teotia, R. S. (1995). Black mildew – A New Disease of Mulberry (*Morus alba* L.). *Indian Phytopathol.*, **48**: 489.

Teotia, R. S. and Mandal, S. K. (1993). Bacterial Leaf Blight Disease of Mulberry. *Indian Silk*, **32**: 41-44.

Teotia, R. S. and Mandal, S. K. (1994). Studies on the Fungicidal Control of Leaf Rust Disease (*Aecidium mori* Berclay) of Mulberry. *Sericologia*, **34**: 555-557.

Teotia, R. S. and Sen, S. K. (1994). Mulberry Diseases in India and their Control. *Sericologia*, **34**: 1-18.

Teotia, R.S.; Kumar, A. and Mandal, S.K. (1992). Biological Control of Powdery Mildew. *Indian Silk*, **31 (1):** 26.

Teotia, R. S.; Mandal, S. K. and Sen, S. K. (1992). Can Root knot Nematodes in Mulberry be Controlled. *Indian Silk*, **30**: 6-9.

Tikader, A. and Thangavelu, K. (2003). Incidence of *Oecophylla smaragdina* (Fabricus) (Hymenoptera: Formicidae) on Mulberry (*Morus* sp.). *Indian J. Seric.*, **42**: 186-187.

Tronsmo, A. (1996). *Trichoderma harzianum* in Biological Control of Fungal Diseases; in *Principles and Practices of Managing Soil Borne Plant Pathogens*. Robert, H. (ed.), pp. 213-235, APS Press, the American Phytopathological Society, St. Paul, Mimesota.

Vander Plank, J. E. (1963). *Plant Diseases: Epidermis and Control*. Academic Press, New York.

Yadav, B. R. D. and Kasturi Bai, A. R. (1988). Cultural Control of Collar-rot Disease of Mulberry (*Morus alba* L.). *Sericologia*, **28**: 261-268.

Yadav, B. R. D. and Saratchandra, B. (1996). *Pestalotiopsis morifolia* sp. on *Morus alba* Var. MR2. *Sericologia*, **36**: 363-366.

Yadav, B. R. D. and Sukumar, J. (1987). Occurrence of a New Stem Blight and Collar-rot Disease of Mulberry from India. *Sericologia*, **27**: 205-206.

Yey, B. and Guz, C. (1990). Chemical Control of Mulberry Thrips, *Pseudodendrothrips mori* (Nawa). *Sericologia*, **30**: 389-392.

Zeya, S. B.; Khan, M. A. and Malik, M. A. (2000). New Record of Insect Pest of Mulberry from Jammu & Kashmir. *Indian J. Seric.*, **39**: 189-192.

Index